CHRISTIAN PARTIES FOR AUTUMN AND WINTER

by Mary McMillan

illustrated by Janet Skiles

Cover by Janet Skiles

Shining Star Publications, Copyright © 1989
A Division of Good Apple, Inc.

ISBN No. 086653-497-0

Printing No. 98765432

Shining Star Publications
A Division of Good Apple, Inc.
Box 299
Carthage, Illinois 62321-0299

A WORD TO PARENTS & TEACHERS

Christian Parties for Autumn and Winter was written with the primary child in mind. The book is made up of thirteen separate celebration/party ideas which include invitations, party hat and place cards, place mats and table decorations, games, crafts, favors and refreshments. Each page is self-explanatory with instructions and/or diagrams. Also each celebration includes verses from the Bible and is based on Christian ideals.

Please remember to never pass out the invitations in a public setting where some children will be left out. If you do not intend to invite all of the children (for instance, in a classroom situation), then mail your invitations. Never forget to think of feelings!

Helpful hint: Gluing is required throughout this book. For the children, glue sticks, liquid glue, paste, etc., are fine. However, for some of the projects (party hats, for example), a hot glue gun would be very helpful. Just remember for safety reasons, do not allow the children to use the glue gun.

Have happy celebrations through our Lord and Savior!

TABLE OF CONTENTS

Shining Star Publications, Copyright © 1989, A division of Good Apple, Inc.   SS1815

FIRST DAY OF AUTUMN

(September 22 or 23. Check your current calendar.)

"To every thing there is a season, and a time to every purpose under the heaven:"

Ecclesiastes 3:1

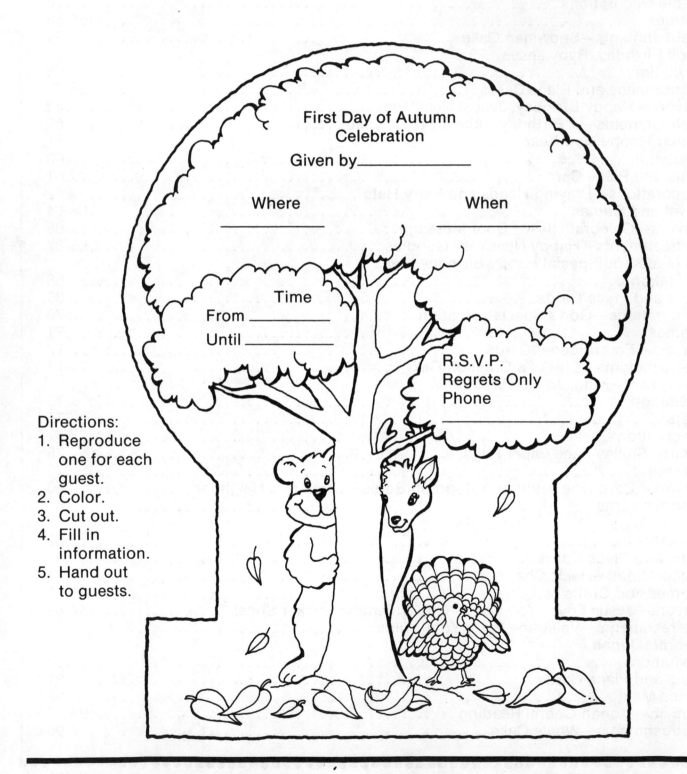

First Day of Autumn
Celebration

Given by_____

Where

_____

When

_____

Time
From _____
Until _____

R.S.V.P.
Regrets Only
Phone

_____

Directions:
1. Reproduce one for each guest.
2. Color.
3. Cut out.
4. Fill in information.
5. Hand out to guests.

SS1815

PLACE MATS WITH TRIVIA QUESTIONS

Trivia Questions and Answers:
1. Who is the bear friend of Eeyore, the donkey? (Winnie the Pooh)
2. In what game might you go to jail? (Monopoly)
3. All the King's horses and all the King's men couldn't do what? (Put Humpty Dumpty back together again.)

Bear:
1. Enlarge to place mat size or attach to place mat size paper.
2. Color.
3. Laminate if possible.
4. Write trivia answers to questions on back of bear.

IF CHILDREN ARE VERY YOUNG, READ QUESTIONS FOR THEM.

Leaves:
1. Cut 2-3 same size as pattern.
2. Color.
3. Write a trivia question on back of each one.
4. Use small piece of masking tape to attach to bear.

*USE PLACE MAT TRIVIA WHILE WAITING FOR REFRESHMENTS.

SS1815

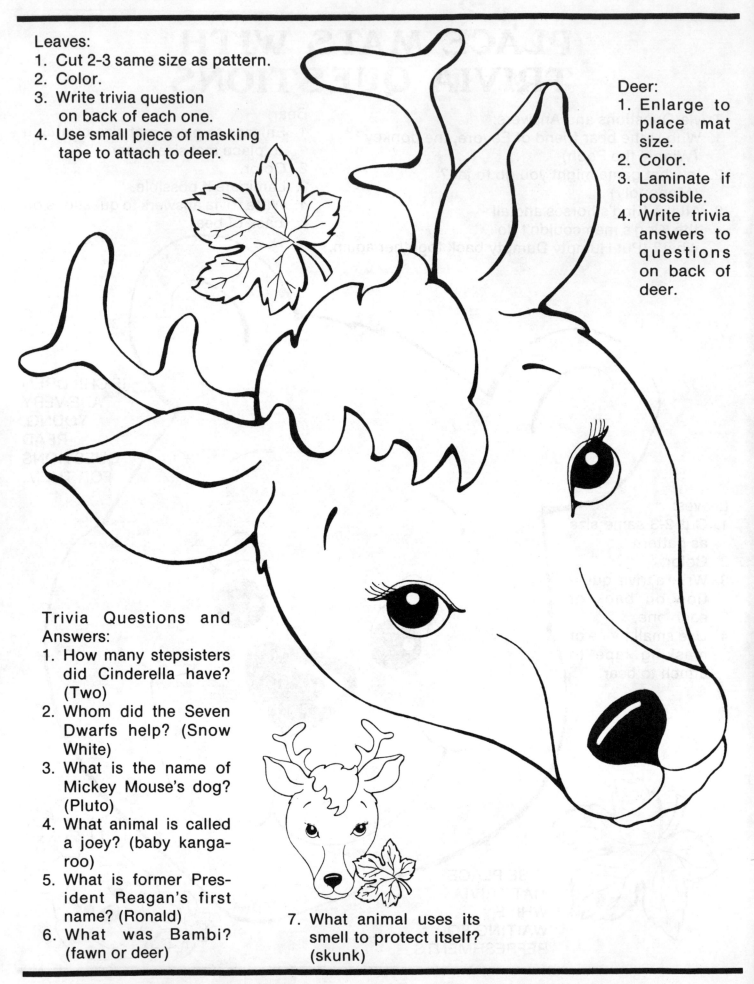

Leaves:
1. Cut 2-3 same size as pattern.
2. Color.
3. Write trivia question on back of each one.
4. Use small piece of masking tape to attach to deer.

Deer:
1. Enlarge to place mat size.
2. Color.
3. Laminate if possible.
4. Write trivia answers to questions on back of deer.

Trivia Questions and Answers:
1. How many stepsisters did Cinderella have? (Two)
2. Whom did the Seven Dwarfs help? (Snow White)
3. What is the name of Mickey Mouse's dog? (Pluto)
4. What animal is called a joey? (baby kangaroo)
5. What is former President Reagan's first name? (Ronald)
6. What was Bambi? (fawn or deer)
7. What animal uses its smell to protect itself? (skunk)

　　　　SS1815

Leaves:
1. Cut 2-3 same size as pattern.
2. Color.
3. Write trivia question on back of each one.
4. Use masking tape to attach to turkey.

Turkey:
1. Enlarge to place mat size or attach to place mat size paper.
2. Color.
3. Laminate if possible.
4. Write trivia answers to questions on back of turkey.

Trivia Questions and Answers:
1. On what TV show do Bert and Ernie appear? (Sesame Street)
2. Where can you buy a hamburger under golden arches? (McDonald's)
3. Who is Ken's girlfriend? (Barbie)
4. Who is Snoopy's 'bird' friend? (Woodstock)
5. What movie was Dorothy in? (Wizard of Oz)
6. Who are Huey, Louie, and Dewey? (Donald Duck's nephews)
7. What friend of Richie wears a black leather jacket? (The Fonz)

SS1815

TABLE DECORATIONS

1. Use a white tablecloth over the party table.
2. Place an orange piece of paper about 2' wide (depending on the width of the table) down the center of the white tablecloth. If orange is not available, be sure to use a fall color.
3. Arrange the place mats with the trivia questions around the tablecloth area for your guests. Then, use the following patterns to make and arrange the table centerpiece.

". . . in that he did good, and gave us rain from heaven, and fruitful seasons, filling our hearts with food and gladness."

Acts 14:17

Bear:

1. Reproduce and color.
2. Cut out on dark line.
3. Fold around and glue dotted areas to make stand.

Fill cup with jelly beans! Be sure to use fall colors—red, yellow, orange, brown, green.

Glue dotted areas to make stand.

Shining Star Publications, Copyright © 1989, A division of Good Apple, Inc.

SS1815

CENTERPIECE

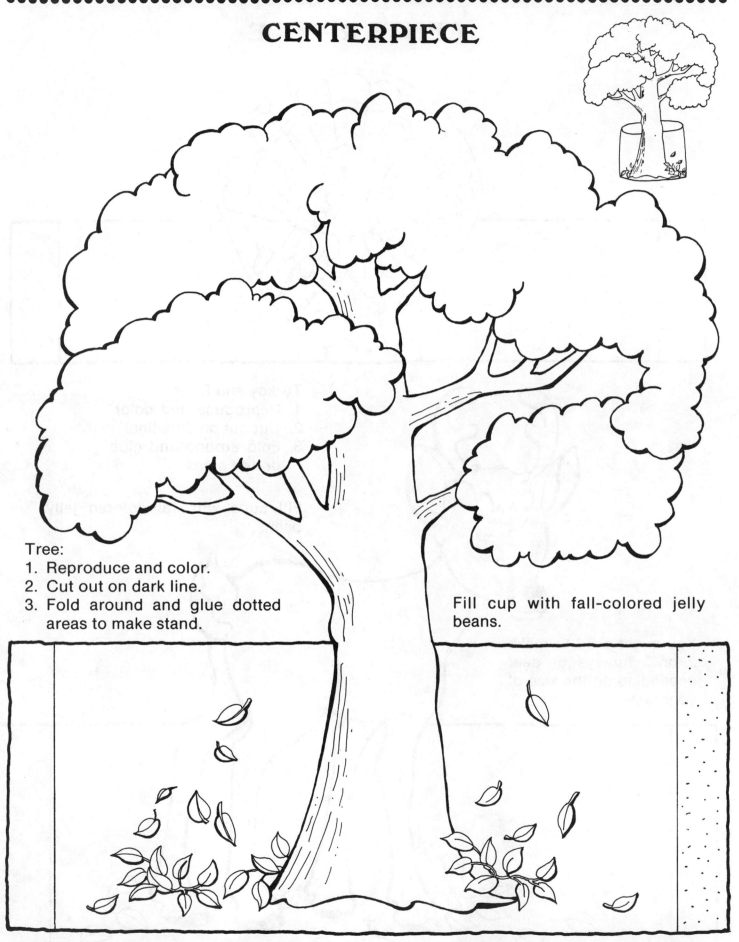

Tree:
1. Reproduce and color.
2. Cut out on dark line.
3. Fold around and glue dotted areas to make stand.

Fill cup with fall-colored jelly beans.

Glue dotted areas to make stand.

SS1815

CENTERPIECE

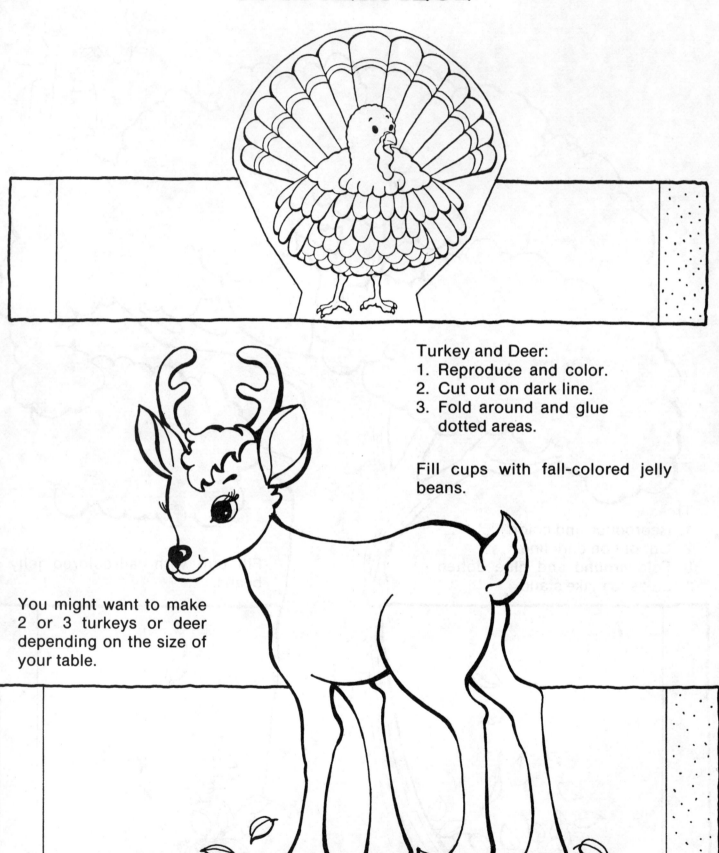

Turkey and Deer:
1. Reproduce and color.
2. Cut out on dark line.
3. Fold around and glue dotted areas.

Fill cups with fall-colored jelly beans.

You might want to make 2 or 3 turkeys or deer depending on the size of your table.

SS1815

GAME
BE A BEAR!

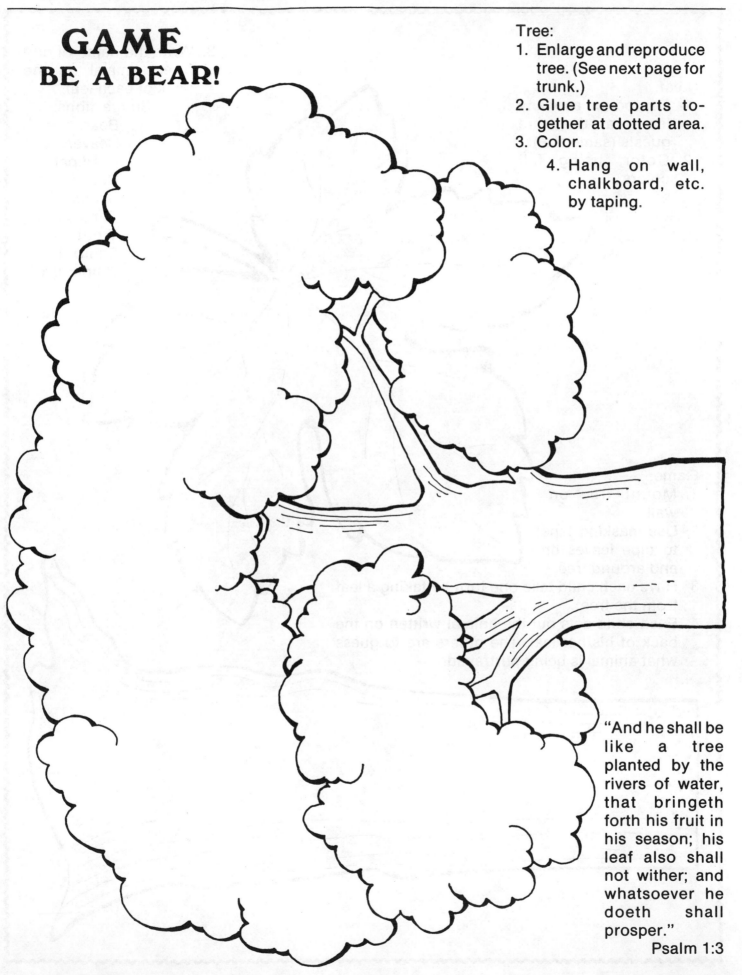

Tree:
1. Enlarge and reproduce tree. (See next page for trunk.)
2. Glue tree parts together at dotted area.
3. Color.
4. Hang on wall, chalkboard, etc. by taping.

"And he shall be like a tree planted by the rivers of water, that bringeth forth his fruit in his season; his leaf also shall not wither; and whatsoever he doeth shall prosper."
Psalm 1:3

SS1815

Leaf:
1. Reproduce as many leaves as there are guests (same size).
2. Color, using fall colors.

3. Write the name of one forest animal on the back of each leaf.
   Suggestions:
   Bear
   Beaver
   Cardinal
   Deer
   Skunk
   Turkey
   Trout
   Squirrel
   Chipmunk

Game:
1. Mount tree on wall.
2. Use masking tape to tape leaves on and around tree.
3. Have each child take one turn by taking a leaf from the tree.
4. Each child acts out the animal written on the back of his/her leaf. The others are to guess what animal is being portrayed.

SS1815

REFRESHMENTS
ANIMAL APPLESAUCE CUPS

Use turkey, deer, and bear patterns to cut and shape the top of plastic cups. Then, fill with applesauce for refreshments.

Serve with chocolate layer cake and milk!

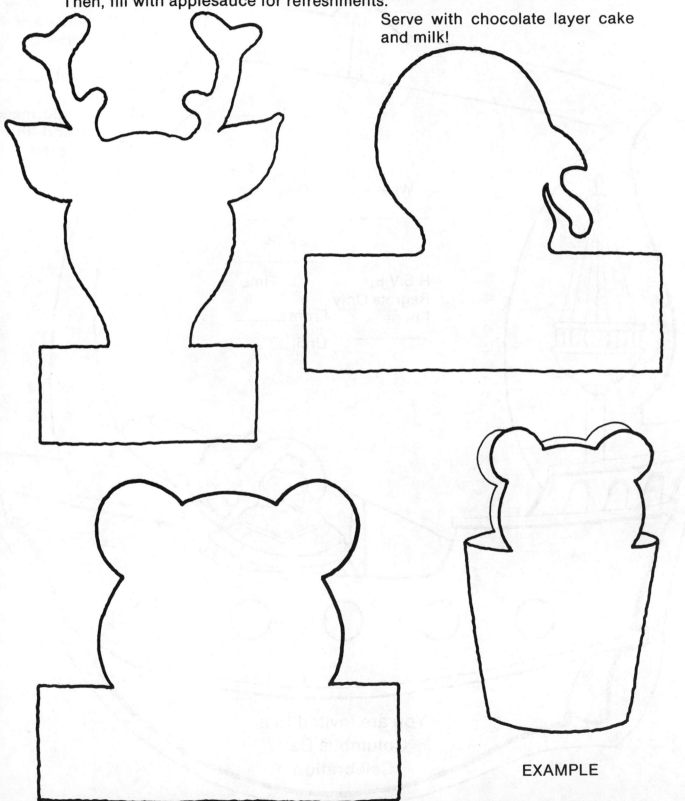

EXAMPLE

SS1815

COLUMBUS DAY

(The second Monday in October)

"And I gave my heart to seek and search out by wisdom concerning all things that are done under heaven: . . ." Ecclesiastes 1:13

Directions:
1. Reproduce one for each guest.
2. Color
3. Cut out on dark line.
4. Fill in information.
5. Hand out to guests.

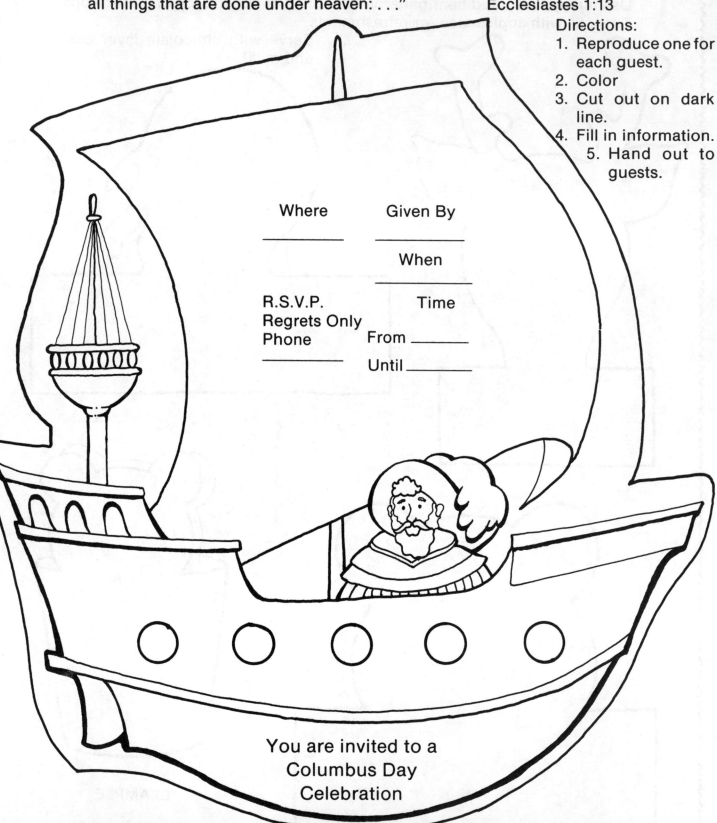

Where _____

Given By _____

When _____

R.S.V.P.
Regrets Only
Phone
_____

Time

From _____

Until _____

You are invited to a
Columbus Day
Celebration

PLACE MATS

1. Enlarge and reproduce the ship pattern on pieces of colored construction paper, or attach to place mat size paper.

2. Use as place mats around the party table.

SS1815

PLACE CARDS

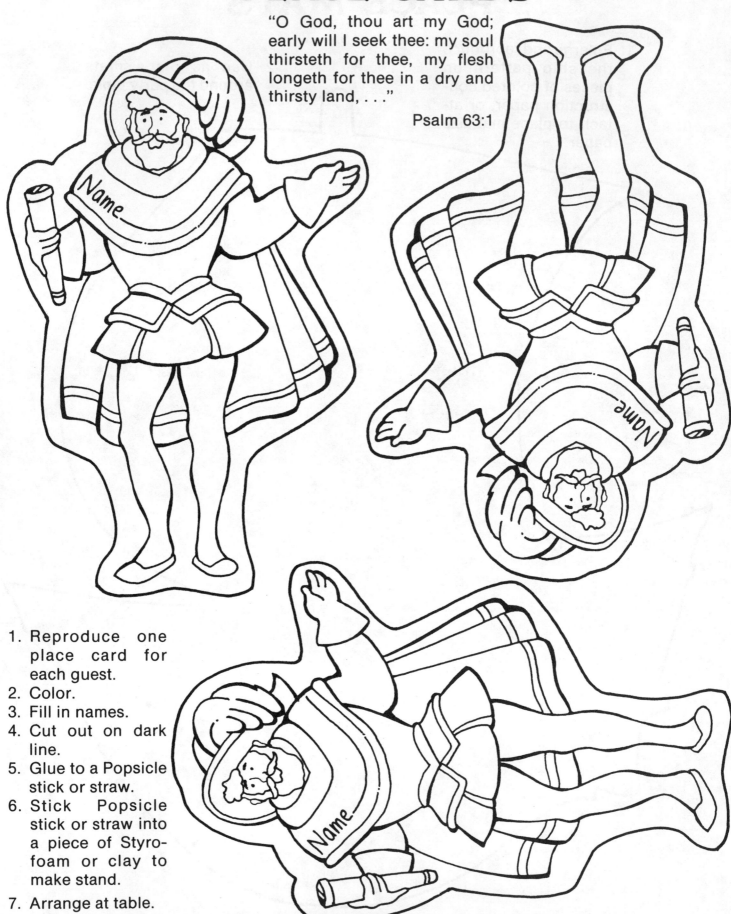

1. Reproduce one place card for each guest.
2. Color.
3. Fill in names.
4. Cut out on dark line.
5. Glue to a Popsicle stick or straw.
6. Stick Popsicle stick or straw into a piece of Styrofoam or clay to make stand.
7. Arrange at table.

GAME
COLUMBUS HAD THREE SHIPS

Columbus had three ships on his first voyage to the New World. They were the Santa María, the Nina, and the Pinta.

Instructions for the Santa María, the Nina, and the Pinta race:

1. Use the pattern from next page to reproduce 3 ships on heavy cardboard or poster board (same size as pattern).

2. Color and cut out. Then, punch hole on mark shown.

3. Use a marker to label one ship the Santa María, another the Nina, and the third the Pinta.

4. Run a string through the punched out hole of each ship. (String should be at least 12' long.)

5. Divide your guests into 3 teams with at least 3 people on each team.

6. Put a member of Team #1 and a member of Team #2 at the end of each string with the ships all at the same starting end.

7. Have the members of Team #3 ready to push each ship down the string toward the finish when a designated person says "Go!"

8. If you have more than nine guests, make it a relay!

9. Of course, the winner is the ship that reaches the end of the string first.

SS1815

"... and we kneeled down on the shore, and prayed."   Acts 21:5

CRAFT

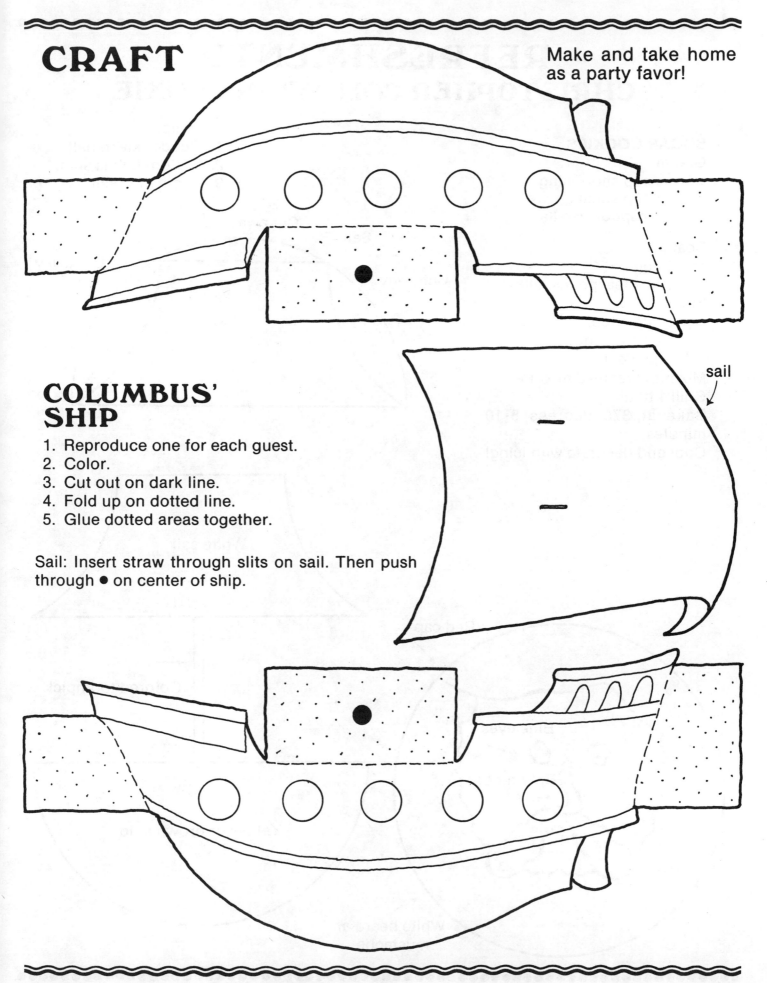

COLUMBUS' SHIP

1. Reproduce one for each guest.
2. Color.
3. Cut out on dark line.
4. Fold up on dotted line.
5. Glue dotted areas together.

Sail: Insert straw through slits on sail. Then push through ● on center of ship.

sail

19

SS1815

REFRESHMENTS
CHRISTOPHER COLUMBUS COOKIE

SUGAR COOKIES
Cream:
    2/3 cup shortening
    3/4 cup sugar
    1 teaspoon vanilla

Beat in:
    1 egg
    3 to 4 teaspoons milk
Sift together:
    2 cups flour
    1½ teaspoons baking
      powder
Mix into creamed mixture.
Chill 1 hour.
Bake at 375 degrees 8-10 minutes.
Cool and decorate with icing!

For ship:
1. Cut cookie in half.
2. Bottom half is ship.
3. Top half is sail.

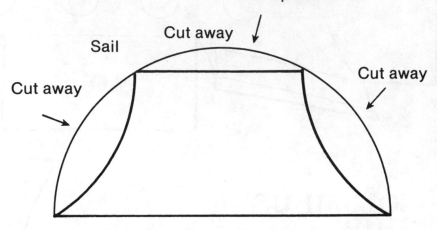

Sail

Cut away

Cut away

Cut away

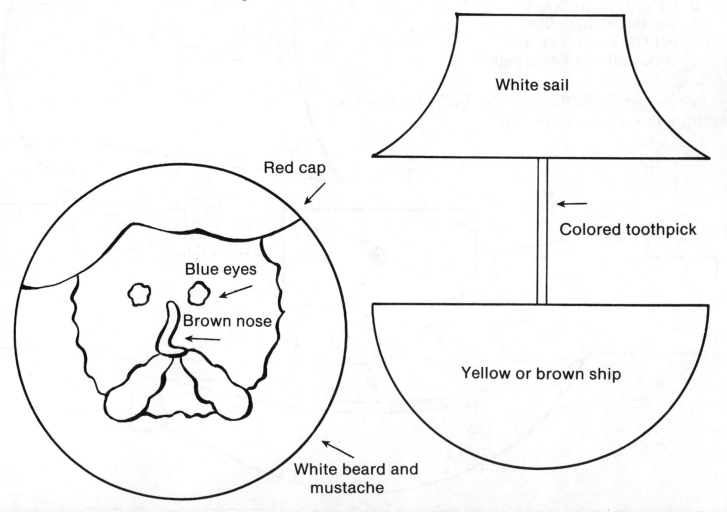

White sail

Colored toothpick

Yellow or brown ship

Red cap

Blue eyes

Brown nose

White beard and mustache

WELCOME HOME FROM THE HOSPITAL

Directions:

1. Reproduce one for each guest.
2. Color.
3. Cut out on dark line.
4. Glue bear shape with party information to inside of card.
5. Fold on dotted line.
6. Hand out to guests.

"My help cometh from the Lord, which made heaven and earth."   Psalm 121:2

Given By

_____

Where _____
When _____
From _____
Until _____
RSVP Regrets Only

_____

fold here ↓

Welcome home from the hospital!
Praise God!

is coming

home!

Come to our party and help us celebrate!

    SS1815

NURSE'S CAP

HAT

1. Reproduce and color.
2. Cut out on dark line.
3. Staple piece #1 across back to form frame.
4. Staple piece #2 into inside of frame.

5. Glue piece #3 to front center of nurse's cap.

place on fold   piece #1

piece #3

place on fold   piece #2

6. Use a bobby pin to attach to hair—(front and back of cap) and to hold in place.

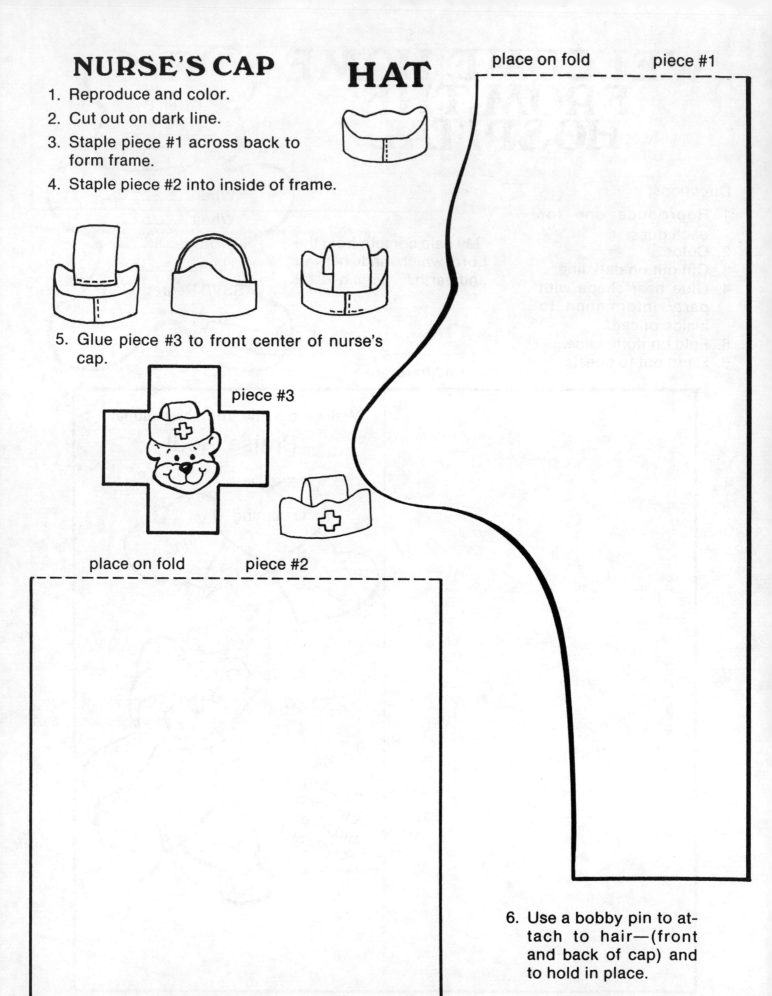

SS1815

PLACE MATS
WELCOME HOME HEART

"And Jesus saith unto him, I will come and heal him." Matthew 8:7

1. Reproduce and color.
2. Cut out on dark line.
3. Arrange the bear parts around the heart as shown in diagram.
4. Use marker to write message in center of heart. Or, use the heart as a place card, too, by writing your guest's names in the center of each to show where they should sit around the table.

Welcome home Eric!

SS1815

DECORATIONS
STUFFED BEARS

1. Reproduce two copies for each bear you make.
2. Color the front side copy and then the back side copy.

Use the pattern given to make stuffed bears!

3. Cut out on dark line.
4. Stuff with newspaper, cotton, tissue, etc.
5. Glue along edges to enclose stuffing.

_____

is home
from the hospital!
Praise God!

Put the bears everywhere to decorate for your party! Hang them from the ceiling, place them around the room, arrange them on the table for a centerpiece. (Great for party favors, too!)

SS1815

FAVORS

BAND-AID STICKER SHEET

Instructions:
1. Reproduce one copy for each guest.
2. Mix equal amounts of Elmer's glue or Lepage's mucilage and water together in a small container.
3. Use a paintbrush and apply the glue mixture to the back of each sticker page.
4. Let the pages dry completely, glue side up.
5. Give as favors at the party and tell your guests to use the stickers to decorate their Band-Aids the next time they need to wear one.

"And Jesus went about all the cities and villages, . . . healing every sickness and every disease among the people." Matthew 9:35

Band-Aid Sticker Sheet: 1. Color. 2. Cut out. 3. Stick to Band-Aids.

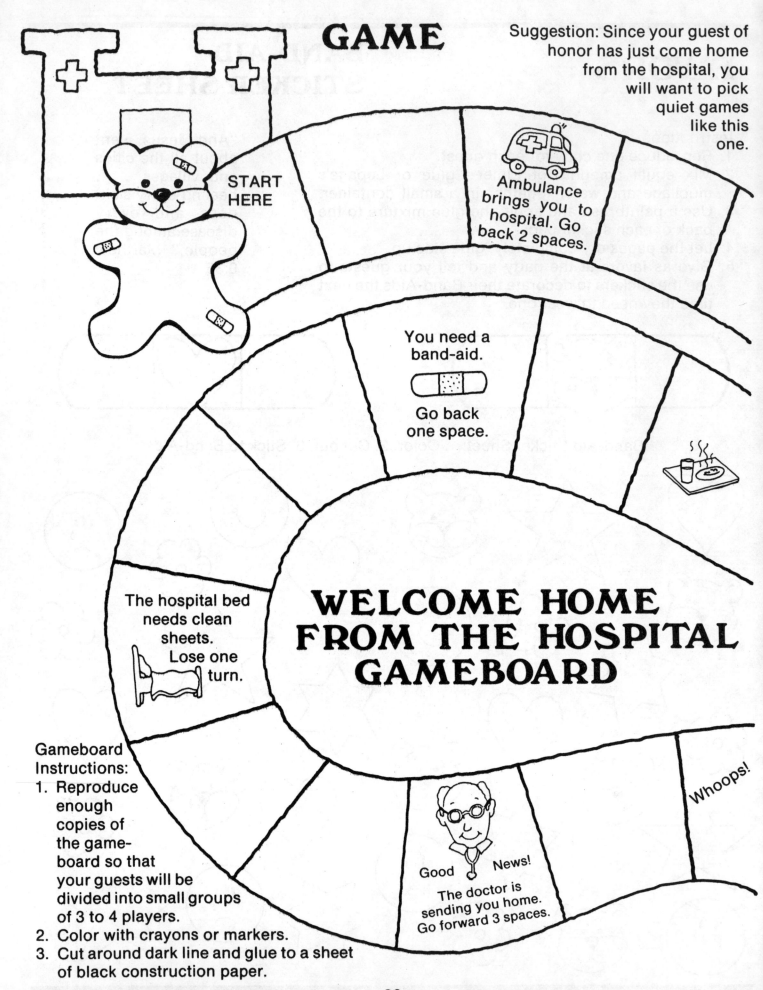

GAME

Suggestion: Since your guest of honor has just come home from the hospital, you will want to pick quiet games like this one.

START HERE

Ambulance brings you to hospital. Go back 2 spaces.

You need a band-aid.

Go back one space.

The hospital bed needs clean sheets. Lose one turn.

WELCOME HOME FROM THE HOSPITAL GAMEBOARD

Whoops!

Good News!

The doctor is sending you home. Go forward 3 spaces.

Gameboard Instructions:
1. Reproduce enough copies of the gameboard so that your guests will be divided into small groups of 3 to 4 players.
2. Color with crayons or markers.
3. Cut around dark line and glue to a sheet of black construction paper.

Shining Star Publications, Copyright © 1989, A division of Good Apple, Inc.

SS1815

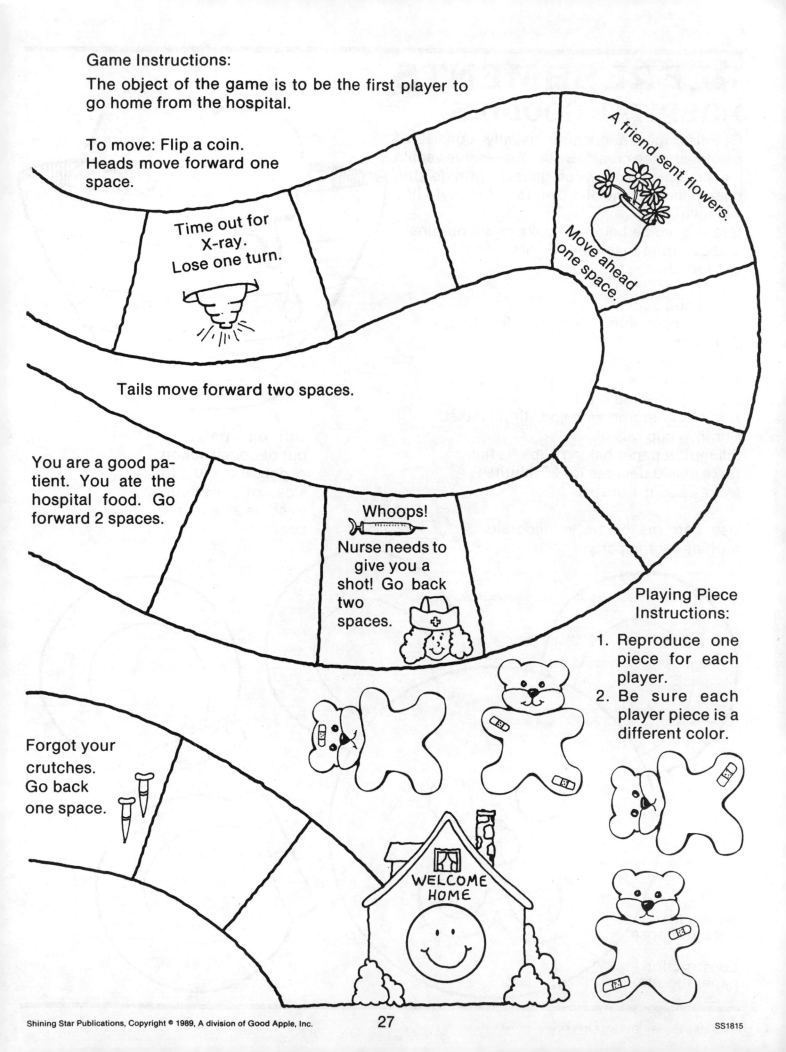

Game Instructions:

The object of the game is to be the first player to go home from the hospital.

To move: Flip a coin. Heads move forward one space.

Time out for X-ray. Lose one turn.

A friend sent flowers. Move ahead one space.

Tails move forward two spaces.

You are a good patient. You ate the hospital food. Go forward 2 spaces.

Whoops! Nurse needs to give you a shot! Go back two spaces.

Playing Piece Instructions:

1. Reproduce one piece for each player.
2. Be sure each player piece is a different color.

Forgot your crutches. Go back one space.

WELCOME HOME

SS1815

REFRESHMENTS
HOSPITAL GOODIES

Goodies in the hospital usually consist of gelatin and ice cream. Be unique—serve vanilla ice cream and let your guests sprinkle dry, cherry-flavored gelatin over top. Yummy! They will love it!

Use the recipe below to make raisin muffins and decorate to look like bears!

Sift together:
    1¾ cups flour
    ¼ cup sugar
    2½ teaspoons baking powder
Combine:
    1 beaten egg
    ¾ cup milk
    ⅓ cup salad oil
Add to dry ingredients and stir till moist.
Stir in ¾ cup raisins.
Fill muffin paper baking cups ⅔ full.
Bake at 400 degrees for 25 minutes
Makes about 1 dozen.

Use patterns below to decorate muffins for the party!

Cut ear patterns out of construction paper and glue to sides of paper cup to serve as ears for bear.

cut slit

raisins for eyes and nose

construction paper mouth

SS1815

ELECTION DAY

(The first Tuesday after the first Monday in November. Check your current calendar.)

"Lead me, O Lord, in thy righteousness because of mine enemies;
make thy way straight before my face."   Psalm 5:8

The Lord allows us to make choices, and because He does, we should try to make good choices. Because we live in a free country, we are privileged in that we are able to choose our own leaders. Let us remember to thank our Lord for this wonderful privilege.

Election Day is the day on which national elections for presidential electors take place.

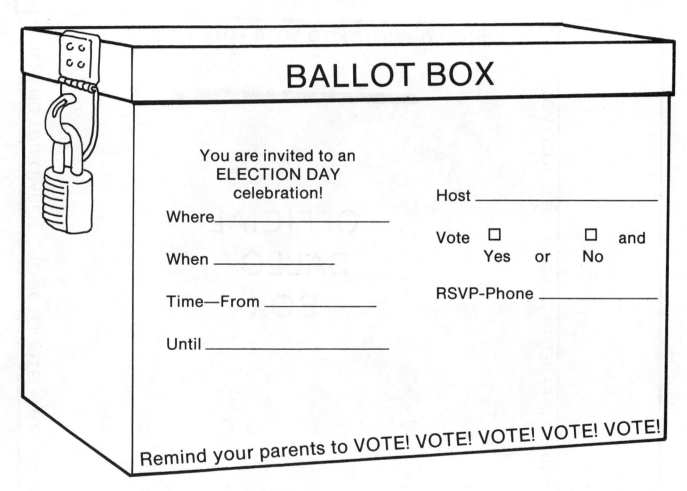

BALLOT BOX

You are invited to an
ELECTION DAY
celebration!

Where_____

When _____

Time—From _____

Until _____

Host _____

Vote ☐   ☐ and
     Yes   or   No

RSVP-Phone _____

Remind your parents to VOTE! VOTE! VOTE! VOTE! VOTE!

Directions:
1. Reproduce one for every guest.
2. Color.
3. Fill in information.
4. Cut out on dark line.
5. Hand out.

✫✫✫✫✫✫✫✫✫✫✫✫✫✫✫✫✫✫✫✫✫✫✫✫✫✫✫✫✫✫✫✫✫✫✫

PLACE MATS

1. Enlarge and reproduce the ballot box pattern on different colors of construction paper.
2. Use as place mats around the party table.

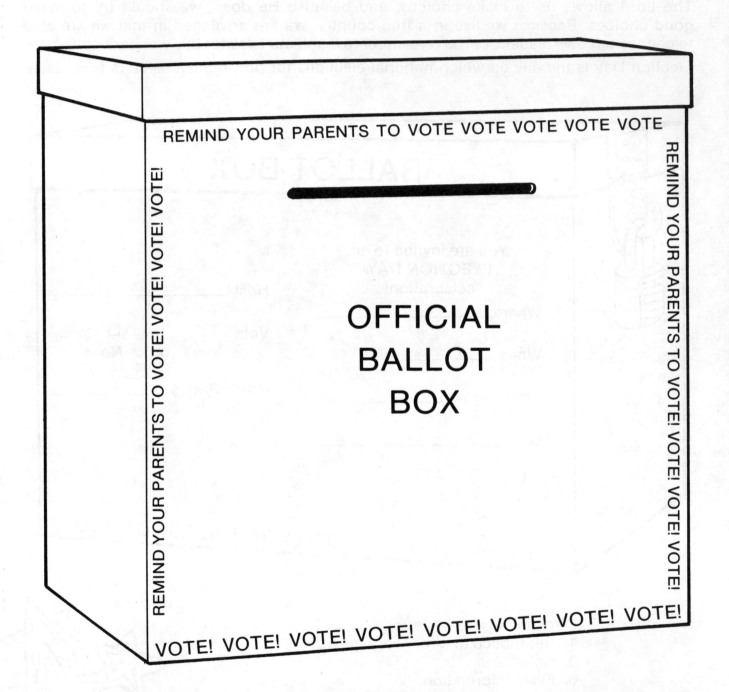

OFFICIAL
BALLOT
BOX

REMIND YOUR PARENTS TO VOTE VOTE VOTE VOTE VOTE

REMIND YOUR PARENTS TO VOTE! VOTE! VOTE! VOTE!

REMIND YOUR PARENTS TO VOTE! VOTE! VOTE! VOTE!

VOTE! VOTE! VOTE! VOTE! VOTE! VOTE! VOTE! VOTE!

"And he said, The God of our fathers hath chosen thee, that thou shouldest know his will, . . ." Acts 22:14

✫✫✫✫✫✫✫✫✫✫✫✫✫✫✫✫✫✫✫✫✫✫✫✫✫✫✫✫✫✫✫✫✫✫✫

SS1815

PLACE CARDS

1. Reproduce one candidate button for each boy and/or girl invited to the party.
2. Color buttons.
3. Glue to heavy cardboard—same size and shape.
4. Tape Popsicle stick to back of button.
5. Take an apple and slice in half.
6. Use apple half as stand by forcing other end of Popsicle stick into the apple.
7. Place around table to arrange seating.

NAPKIN DECORATIONS

1. Reproduce the campaign buttons.   2. Color.   3. Glue to napkins and arrange around table.

ACTIVITY SHEET
TIME TO VOTE

1. Reproduce one ballot for each child.
2. Have the guests look over the ballot.
3. Ask for one volunteer for each cate-
gory to make a campaign speech.
4. Vote by secret ballot.
5. Have someone count the votes and see who wins.

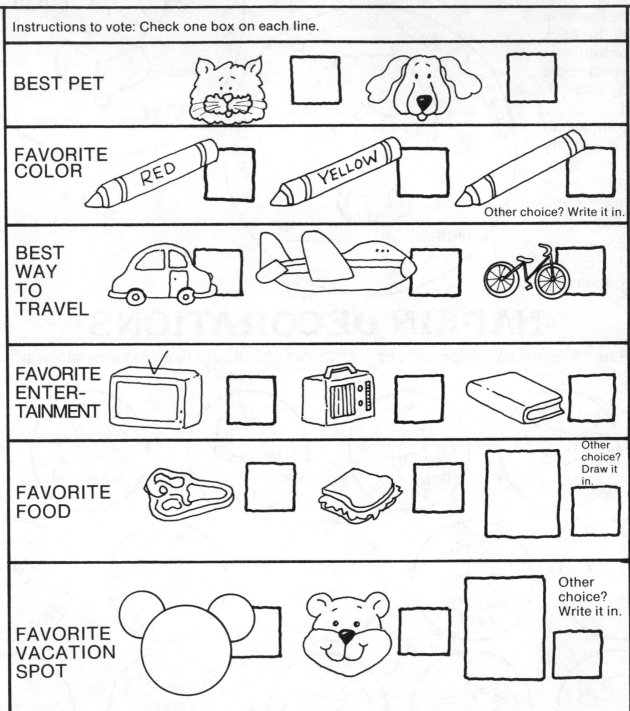

OFFICIAL BALLOT

Instructions to vote: Check one box on each line.

BEST PET

FAVORITE COLOR — RED — YELLOW — Other choice? Write it in.

BEST WAY TO TRAVEL

FAVORITE ENTERTAINMENT — Other choice? Draw it in.

FAVORITE FOOD

FAVORITE VACATION SPOT — Other choice? Write it in.

VOTE! VOTE! VOTE! VOTE! VOTE! VOTE! VOTE! VOTE! VOTE! VOTE! VOTE! VOTE! VOTE! VOTE! VOTE! VOTE! VOTE! VOTE! VOTE!

VOTE! VOTE! VOTE! VOTE! VOTE! VOTE! VOTE! VOTE! VOTE! VOTE! VOTE! VOTE! VOTE! VOTE! VOTE! VOTE! VOTE! VOTE!

SS1815

REFRESHMENTS
VOTE FOR YOUR OWN TOPPING!

This party is a celebration of being able to make choices. Serve a slice of pound cake to each guest and then provide 3 or 4 choices of toppings.
Have each child decide for himself. Then top it off with a non-dairy whipped topping.

A Simple Pound Cake Recipe

1. Cream: 1 stick margarine
   ¾ cup shortening
   3 cups sugar

2. Beat in:
   6 eggs—one at a time
3. Add:
   1 cup milk
   3 cups flour
   1 tablespoon vanilla

4. Beat well for 5 minutes.

5. Pour into a greased and floured bundt pan.

6. Bake at 325 degrees for 1½ hours.

7. Cool and remove from pan.

Choices for Toppings

chocolate chip cookies

fresh strawberries

blueberries

peaches

peanut butter

raspberries

applesauce

ice cream
any flavor

bananas

THANKSGIVING DAY

(The fourth Thursday in November)

"Enter into his gates with thanksgiving, and into his courts with praise: be thankful unto him, and bless his name." Psalm 100:4

Directions:
1. Reproduce one for each guest.
2. Color.
3. Cut out.

4. Fill in information.
5. Deliver.

THANKSGIVING
CELEBRATION

Given By:

_____

Where _____   Time: From _____ Until _____
When _____   RSVP Regrets Only-Phone _____

SS1815

PLACE MATS

1. Reproduce one for each guest.
2. Place around party table.
3. Provide each child with crayons or markers.

4. Instruct the children to color their own place mat and to write in for what they are thankful. (Small children can draw pictures.)

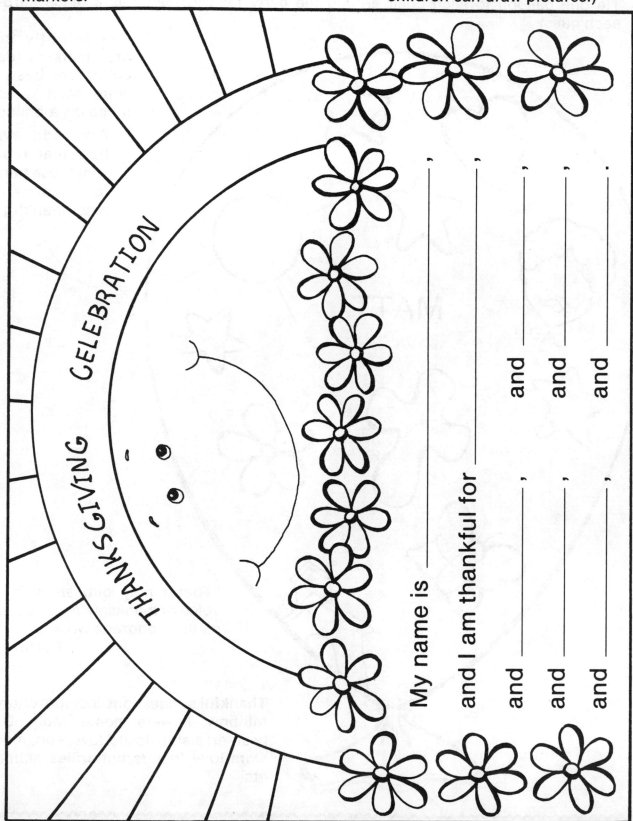

BALLOON PLACE CARDS

1. Purchase rainbow-colored balloons filled with helium. (Remember, balloons will only hold the helium 8-10 hours. Check with your local party supply store and arrange to pick up the balloons a few hours before the party.)
2. Tie one balloon to each chair around the party table to serve as a place card for each guest.

3. Use brightly colored markers (dark colors are best) to write each guest's name on a balloon.

4. Also add symbols that represent those things for which we are most thankful.

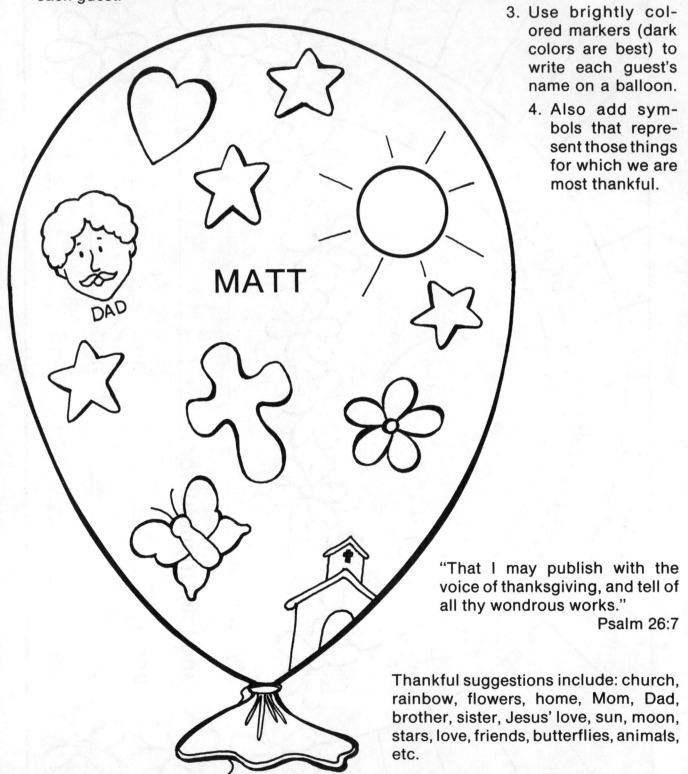

"That I may publish with the voice of thanksgiving, and tell of all thy wondrous works."
Psalm 26:7

Thankful suggestions include: church, rainbow, flowers, home, Mom, Dad, brother, sister, Jesus' love, sun, moon, stars, love, friends, butterflies, animals, etc.

SS1815

CRAFT
MAKE YOUR OWN FILMSTRIP
Have your guests make their own filmstrip depicting symbols of those things for which they are most thankful.

You will need:
1. 2-3 slide jackets (cardboard frames for slides) for each guest. (You can purchase these at any photography supply store.)
2. Several pieces of regular transparency sheets.
3. Enough colored Vis-à-Vis markers for your guests to share. (You might experiment with other types of markers, but the Vis-à-Vis markers work well.)

<table>
<tr>
<td>slide jacket</td>
<td>transparency sheet</td>
<td></td>
</tr>
</table>

Procedure:
1. Give each child a piece of paper with pre-drawn squares—same size as transparency slot in slide jacket. Have the children practice drawing symbols of those things for which they are most thankful. Suggestions: church, butterfly, Mom, Dad, love (heart), etc.

2. When the children are ready, give each one 2-3 slide jackets. (Prepare the slides before party time by cutting transparency squares and fitting them into jackets.)

3. Instruct the children to use the Vis-à-Vis markers and draw in symbols. When all are finished, show on filmstrip projector. Add music for a great effect.

SS1815

ACTIVITY
A THANKSGIVING PLAY

On Thanksgiving Day, people in the United States give thanks to our Lord with feasting and prayer for the many blessings they have received during the year. The first New England Thanksgiving was celebrated by the Pilgrims along with the Indians to thank God for the corn harvest.

Use the following play and character patterns to get into the real spirit of Thanksgiving!

Time: In 1621

Place: In the colony of Massachusetts

Characters: Pilgrim boys   Indian boys   (The number may vary.
Pilgrim girls   Indian girls   Just be sure that you have a part for each guest.)

Pilgrim boy #1: (*The boy walks to center stage with several Indian children following him.*) Come. Everyone come. I have news, and friends for you to meet.

Pilgrim girl #1: (*The Pilgrim girl along with other Pilgrim children gather around the boy and the Indians. All of the Pilgrim children stare at the Indians whom the Pilgrims rarely see up close.*) What is it, John? What is your news?

Pilgrim boy #1: Governor Bradford has declared that a three-day feast will be held to celebrate and give prayers for the corn harvest.

SS1815

Pilgrim boy #2: Oh, that's not news, John. Why, my mother has been preparing for the feast for days by baking cornmeal bread and roasting the duck that my father brought in from the woods.

Pilgrim girl #2: Yes, and my mother is baking apples and preparing a goose.

Pilgrim girl #3: (*Speaks up quickly.*) And my father has caught fish and roasted corn.

Pilgrim boy #3: (*He cannot take his eyes off the Indians.*) Who are your friends, John?

Pilgrim boy #1: The Indian boys and girls came with their families to help celebrate the harvest. Father said we should welcome our new friends.

Pilgrim children: (*Each boy and girl speaks to the Indian children in a friendly manner.*) Welcome. Welcome to our Thanksgiving celebration.

Pilgrim girl #1: (*Speaks to the Indian children.*) I am thankful that you have joined us for our feast.

Indians: (*All of the Indian children smile in friendship.*)

Pilgrim boy #4: Hurry, everyone hurry. My mother is serving her fresh baked pumpkin pie.

(*The Pilgrim children join hands with the Indian children, and they all run offstage for pumpkin pie.*)

Play Character Patterns

See the following page for character patterns. Enlarge the patterns so that the center will fit over a child's face. Color with markers, cut out on dark line, and glue to a Popsicle stick, tongue depressor or dowel stick to serve as a handle.

Be sure to reproduce one for every guest. Have children hold their costumes over their face to represent characters chosen to play.

PLAY CHARACTER PATTERNS

Pilgrim Boy

Pilgrim Girl

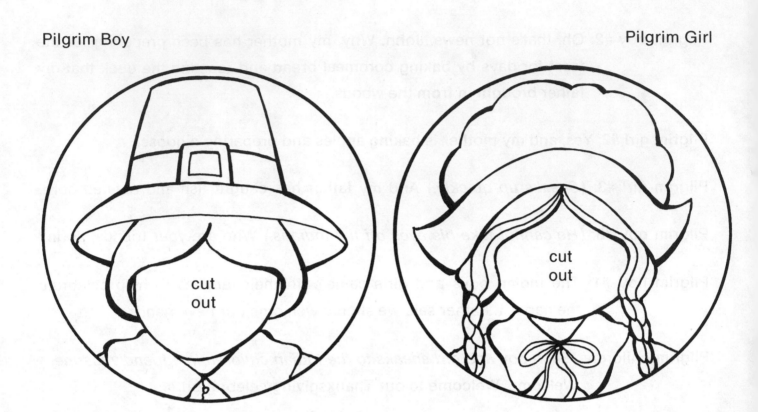

"Offer unto God thanksgiving; and pay
thy vows unto the most High:"
Psalm 50:14

Indian Boy

Indian Girl

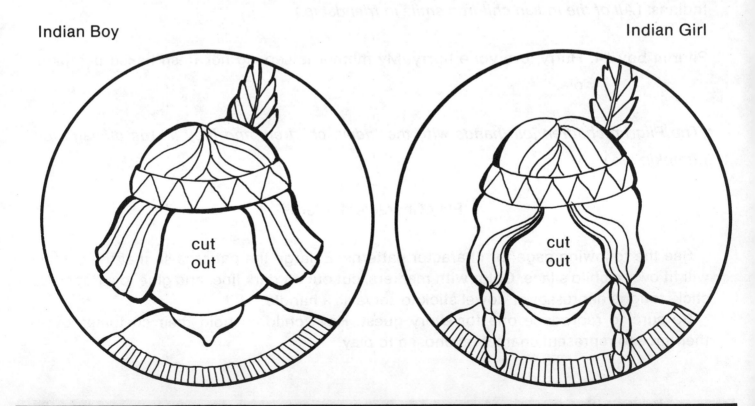

REFRESHMENTS
SUN CAKE

Bake your favorite cake in a large round pan. Let cool. Cut in half.

Ice one half with bright yellow icing to represent the sun. Add raisins, chocolate chip pieces, or dots of chocolate icing to represent eyes. Draw the mouth with chocolate icing that comes in a tube with decorating tips.

RAINBOW CAKE

Ice the other half with red, yellow, blue, violet and white to represent rainbow. (Check directions on food coloring box to make violet color.)

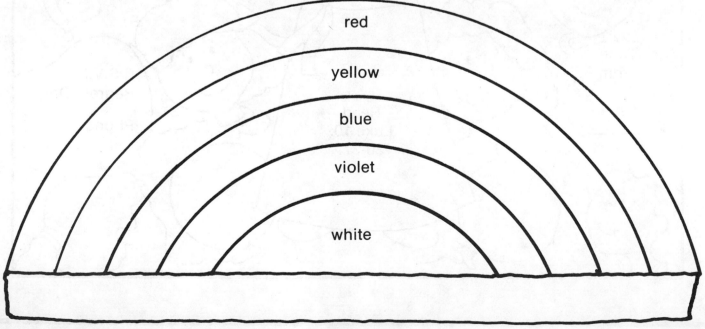

red

yellow

blue

violet

white

SS1815

BE A GOOD SAMARITAN

"... Then said Jesus unto him, Go, and do thou likewise."

Luke 10:37

Directions:
1. Reproduce one for each guest.
2. Color.
3. Cut out.
4. Hand out.

PLACE MATS

1. Enlarge pattern so that a small 7" paper plate will fit in center. Reproduce one for each guest.
2. Color with bright markers.
3. Cut out on dark line.
4. Place around table.

Hint:
Use paper plates that are same color as Good Samaritan's gown.

". . . but that the members should have the same care one for another."
I Corinthians 12:25

Hint: Place a small piece of tape on underside of paper plate to hold in place.

Place paper plate here

BE A GOOD SAMARITAN

SS1815

ACTIVITY

Hint:
See
following
page for the
Good
Samaritan
award.

1. Reproduce one for each guest.
2. Provide crayons and pencils and have the children check the lists together. Add their own ideas to the back. Then instruct them to go home and complete it.

MY GOOD SAMARITAN CHECKLIST

Instructions: Check those things that you can do to be a Good Samaritan.

☐ ♥ THY NEIGHBOR

☐ HELP SOMEONE WHO IS

☐ AND BE FRIENDLY TO EVERYONE

☐ BE KIND TO

☐ WORK HARD IN School

☐ MAKE NEW NEIGHBORS FEEL WELCOME

☐ HELP A FRIEND LEARN TO

☐ HELP DAD CLEAN THE YARD

☐ SHARE YOUR

SS1815

FAVORS

Present one to each guest with instructions for their parents to award them after they have proudly completed their Good Samaritan Checklist.

1. Color with bright markers.   2. Cut out on dark line.

THE GOOD SAMARITAN AWARD

is

presented

to

_____

by

_____ (parents)

for
completing
THE GOOD
SAMARITAN
CHECKLIST

School

Church

"Be kindly affectioned one to another
with brotherly love; . . ."
Romans 12:10

Shining Star Publications, Copyright © 1989, A division of Good Apple, Inc.

SS1815

REFRESHMENTS
GOOD "LITTLE" SAMARITAN TREATS!

Serve two types of cookies, popcorn balls and their favorite fruit-flavored drink.

GUMDROP COOKIES

Cream: 1 cup margarine
1½ cups confectioners' sugar
1 teaspoon vanilla

Beat in: 1 egg

Sift together: 2½ cups flour
1 teaspoon baking soda
1 teaspoon cream of tartar

Add to creamed mixture and blend. Divide dough in half. Shape each into a roll. Wrap in waxed paper and chill several hours. Slice.
Place gumdrop on top of each cookie. Bake at 375 degrees for 12 minutes.

POPCORN BALLS

Butter sides of saucepan.
Combine:
2 cups granulated sugar
1½ cups water
½ cup light corn syrup
1 teaspoon vinegar

Cook to 250 degrees to hard ball stage.
Add ½ teaspoon vanilla.
Pour over 5 quarts popped corn.
Shape into balls and serve.

CHOCOLATE COOKIES

Cream: ½ cup shortening
1²/₃ cups granulated sugar
2 teaspoons vanilla
Beat in: 2 eggs
2—1 ounce squares (melted) unsweetened chocolate
Sift: 2 cups flour
2 teaspoons baking powder
Add to creamed mixture.

Add: ⅓ cup milk
Mix.
Chill several hours.

Roll balls in confectioners' sugar.

Bake at 350 degrees for 15 minutes.

                    SS1815

FIRST DAY OF WINTER

(December 21 or 22. Check your current calendar.)

"While the earth remaineth, seedtime and harvest, and cold and heat, and summer and winter, and day and night shall not cease."

Genesis 8:22

Directions:
1. Reproduce one for each guest.
2. Color.
3. Cut out on dark line.
4. Fill out information.

5. Cut door and window open along dark line. Be sure to leave one side of each uncut.
6. Glue door and window onto back side of invitation. Be sure to center each over opening.
7. Hand out to guests.

You
Are
Invited

(Open door and window to read information.)

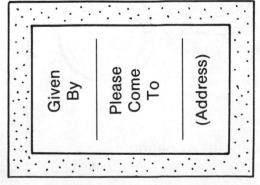

Given By | Please Come To | (Address)

When _____
Time: From _____
Until _____
R.S.V.P.-Regrets Only
Phone_____

Shining Star Publications, Copyright © 1989, A division of Good Apple, Inc.

SS1815

HATS

1. Reproduce one for every guest.
2. Color.
3. Cut out on dark line.
4. Glue back headband to front headband to fit.

First Day of Winter Celebration

PLACE CARDS

1. Reproduce one for each guest.
2. Color.
3. Cut out on dark line.
4. Tape to small paper cup.
5. Fill paper cup with assorted small candies or peanuts.
6. Arrange around table.

My name is

My name is

SS1815

PLACE MATS

1. Reproduce one for every guest. Enlarge to place mat size or attach to place mat size paper.
2. Color.
3. Cut out on dark line.
4. Laminate, if available, for reuse.
5. Arrange around table.

TABLE DECORATIONS

To make table decoration:

1. Reproduce 3 patterns of snowmen.
2. Color.
3. Cut out on dark line.
4. Glue along each inside dotted edge so that the patterns are glued together and made to stand.

Stand your snowmen in the center of the table and arrange cotton around them to represent snow.

"He giveth snow like wool: . . ."
Psalm 147:16

SS1815

GAMES

WINTER RELAY

1. Fill two large sacks with winter clothes, such as:

mittens	winter coat
knitted cap	wool pants
sweater	snow boots
earmuffs	ski pants

2. Divide guests into two relay teams.

3. When designated person says to begin, the first person in each relay team runs to the sack, pulls something out and puts it on. All buttons must be buttoned, and all zippers zipped before person runs back to tag second person in line. Play continues until everyone in line has had a turn. First team finished wins game.

SNOWBALL EATING RELAYS

Use an ice cream dipper to place snowball shaped ice cream dips into individual bowls. Put out as many bowls as contestants have volunteered to participate on each relay team. When designated person says to begin, the first person in each relay begins to eat ice cream with hands behind his back. (No forks, spoons or hands may be used.) When first person on relay team finishes his/her ice cream, second person begins. First team that finishes ice cream wins game.

WINTER ITEMS TO HUNT AND TRADE

1. Reproduce the winter items found on the next page onto construction paper.
2. Hide the items around the party area before your guests arrive.
3. When you are ready to play the game, explain that the different items are worth different values, but that you will not tell what the values are until after the game is over.
4. Instruct the guests to begin, find the objects, and do all the trading they want during game time.
5. After about 15 minutes, stop the trading. Reveal the values and total each guest's score to see who wins. (Be sure to hide three to four sets of each item so that each guest ends up with several items.)

Shining Star Publications, Copyright © 1989, A division of Good Apple, Inc. SS1815

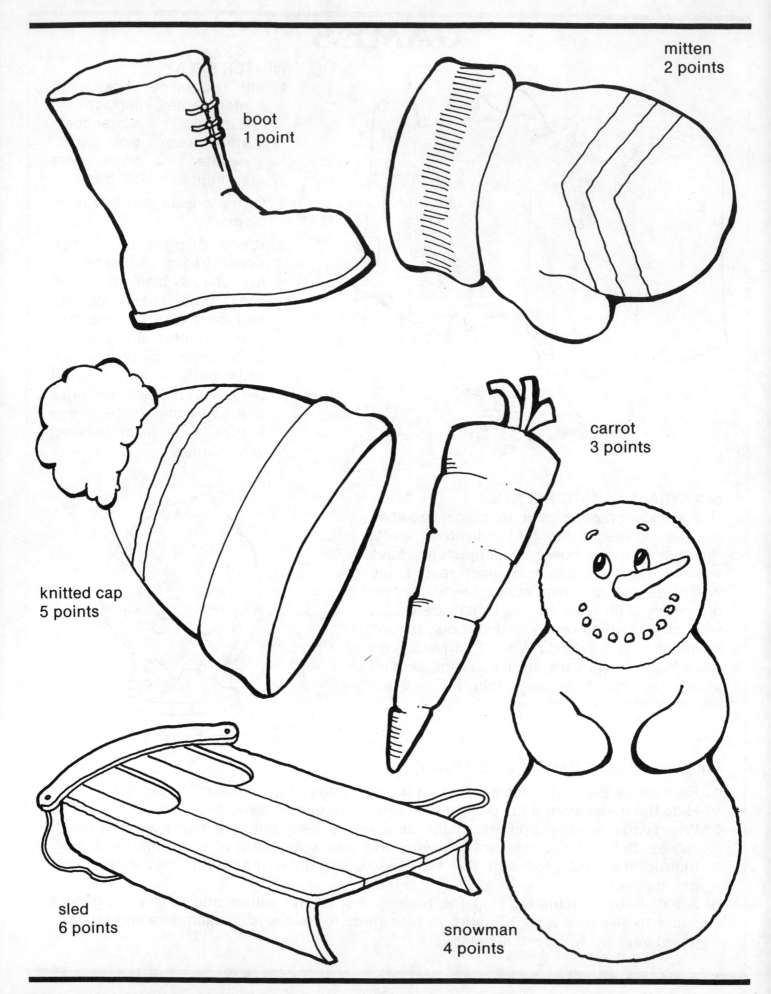

mitten
2 points

boot
1 point

carrot
3 points

knitted cap
5 points

sled
6 points

snowman
4 points

SS1815

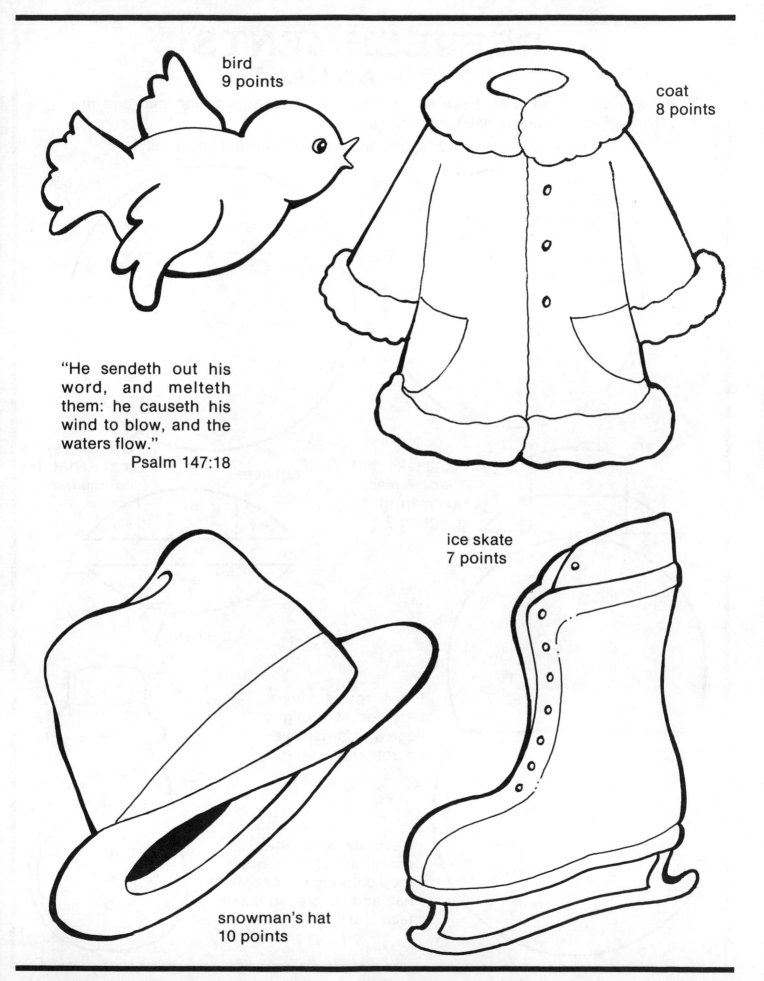

bird
9 points

coat
8 points

"He sendeth out his word, and melteth them: he causeth his wind to blow, and the waters flow."
Psalm 147:18

ice skate
7 points

snowman's hat
10 points

SS1815

REFRESHMENTS
SNOWMAN CAKE

Bake your favorite cake. Bake half of the cake in a large round pan and the other half in a slightly smaller round pan, if available.

Let cool, remove from pans and cut along dotted line area.

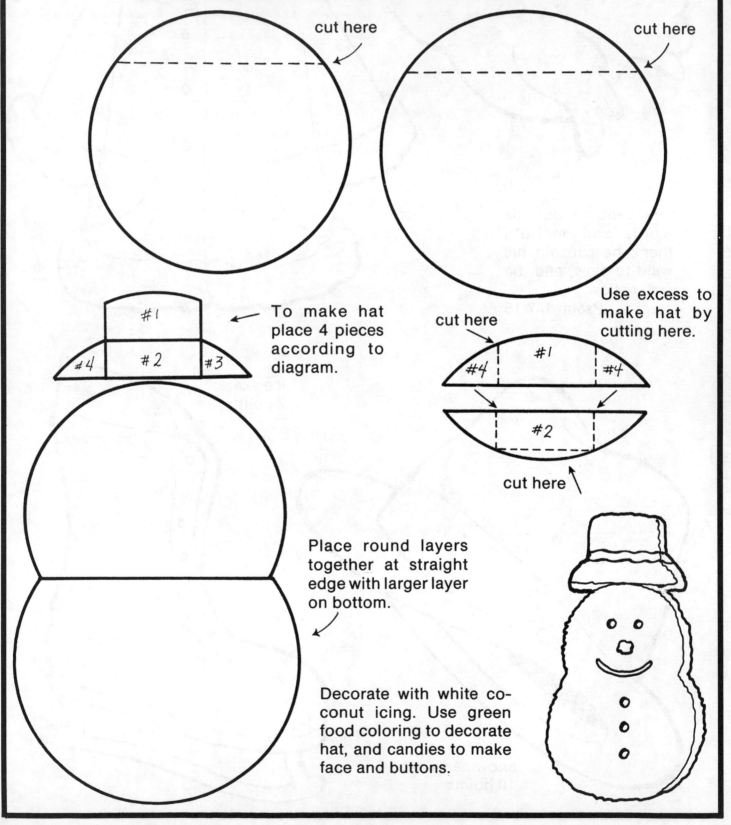

cut here

cut here

To make hat place 4 pieces according to diagram.

#1

#4   #2   #3

cut here

Use excess to make hat by cutting here.

#4   #1   #4

#2

cut here

Place round layers together at straight edge with larger layer on bottom.

Decorate with white coconut icing. Use green food coloring to decorate hat, and candies to make face and buttons.

SS1815

HAPPY BIRTHDAY, BABY JESUS

(Christmas—December 25th)

Let us come together in friendship to rejoice and celebrate the birth of Christ!

"For unto you is born this day in the city of David a Saviour, which is Christ the Lord."

Luke 2:11

You are invited
to a
Birthday Party
for
Baby Jesus

Given By _____

Where _____

When _____

From_____ Until_____

To RSVP—cut out angel, check yes or no, sign name and return to sender.

yes   no

Name

Directions:

1. Reproduce one for each guest. 2. Color, fill in information and cut out. 3. Roll up like a scroll. 4. Tie with red, green, or gold ribbon and hand out.

Shining Star Publications, Copyright © 1989, A division of Good Apple, Inc.   SS1815

CENTERPIECE AND PLACE CARDS

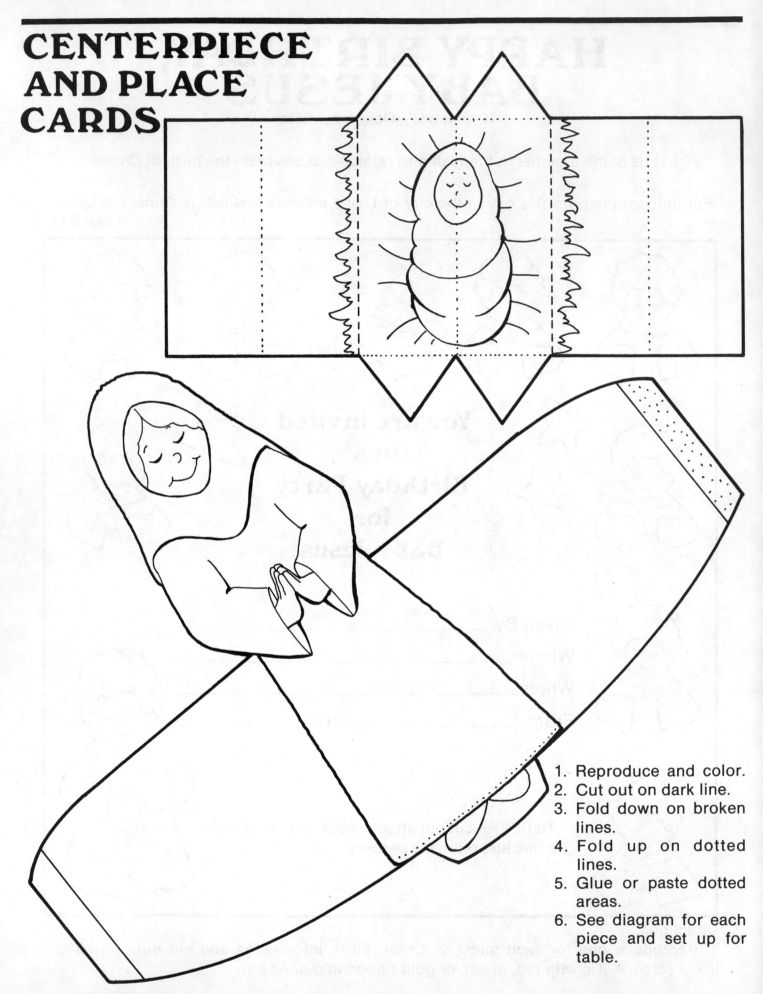

1. Reproduce and color.
2. Cut out on dark line.
3. Fold down on broken lines.
4. Fold up on dotted lines.
5. Glue or paste dotted areas.
6. See diagram for each piece and set up for table.

56

SS1815

sheep

cow

donkey

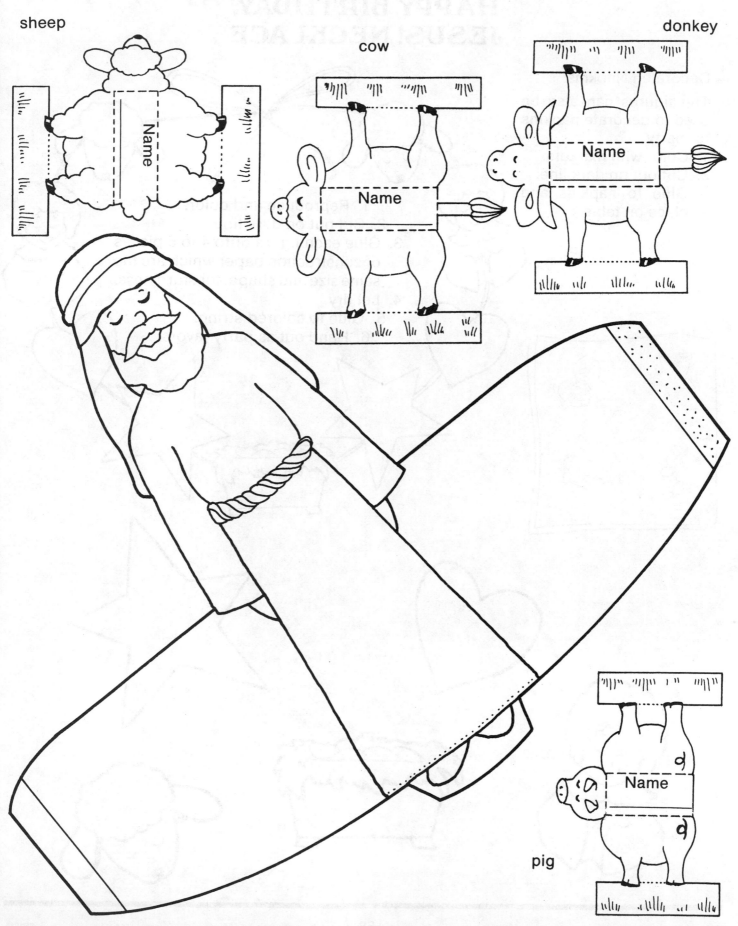

Name

Name

Name

pig

Name

SS1815

FAVORS
HAPPY BIRTHDAY, JESUS! NECKLACE

Decorated Napkins:

The figures can also be used to decorate napkins for party.

1. Color with markers.
2. Cut out on dark line.
3. Glue to napkins and place on table.

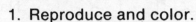

1. Reproduce and color.
2. Cut out on dark line.
3. Glue each figure onto 4 to 5 pieces of construction paper which are the same size and shape, for sturdiness.
4. Let dry.
5. Glue to colored string.
6. Hand out as party favors.

SS1815

REFRESHMENTS
A BIRTHDAY CAKE FOR BABY JESUS

Bake a three-layer round cake of any flavor.
Ice the cake with white icing.
Then, decorate:
1. Color the angels and the star with markers.
2. Cut out on dark line.
3. Carefully slide a toothpick through each figure where the holes indicate.

4. Arrange angels and the star on top of the cake. See diagram.

". . . and he called his name Jesus."
Matthew 1:25

SS1815

ANOTHER HAPPY NEW YEAR

(New Year's Day—January 1)

HAPPY

NEW YEAR

PARTY

"Jesus Christ the same yesterday, and today, and for ever."

Hebrews 13:8

Who _____

Where _____

When _____

From _____

Until _____

RSVP
Regrets Only—Phone

_____

Directions: 1. Reproduce one for each guest. 2. Color 3. Cut out. 4. Fill out information.
5. Hand out.

SS1815

HATS AND PLACE CARDS

1. Reproduce.   2. Color.
3. Cut out.   4. Fit to back headband.

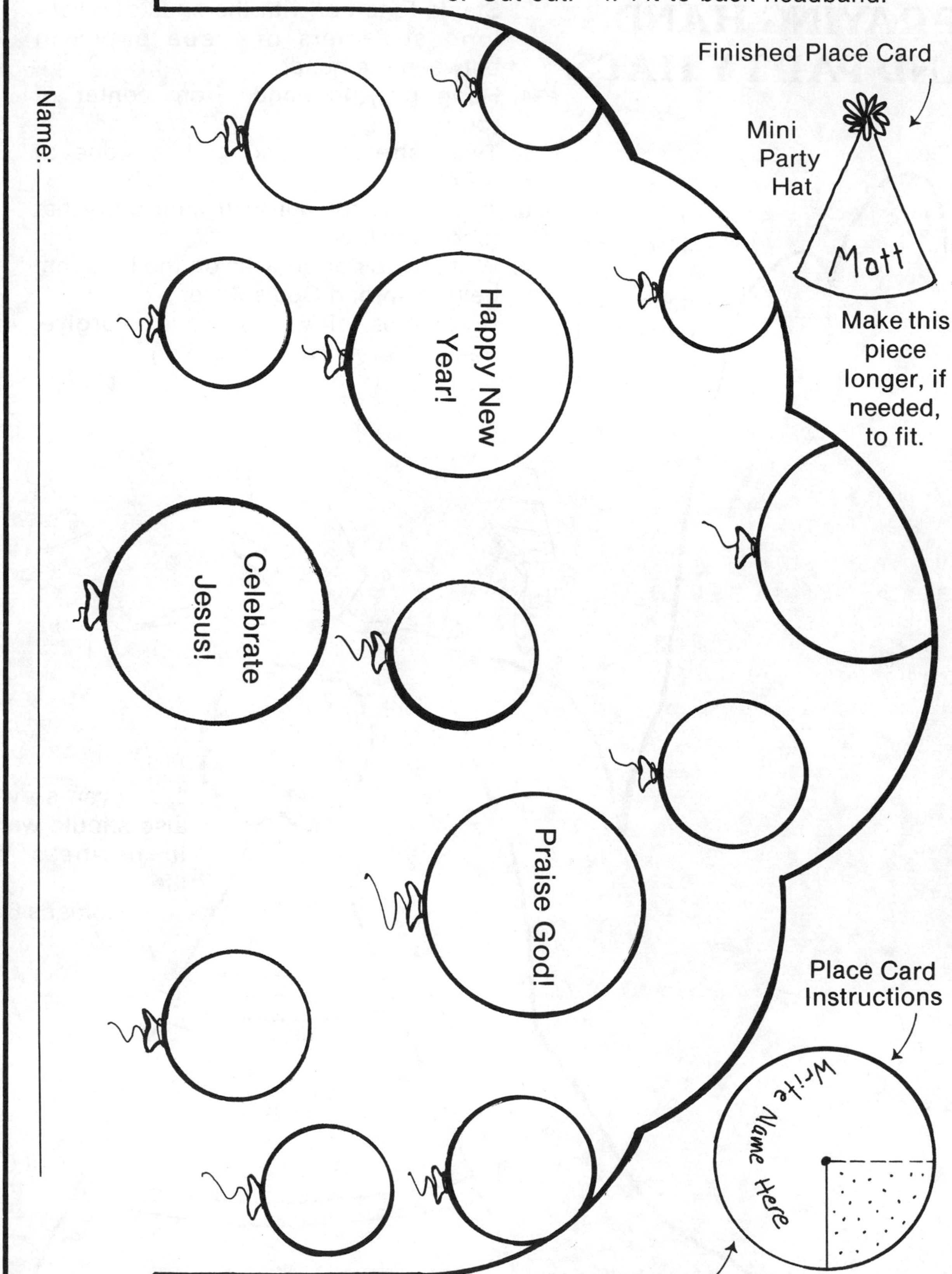

Finished Place Card

Mini
Party
Hat

Matt

Make this
piece
longer, if
needed,
to fit.

Name: _____

Happy New
Year!

Celebrate
Jesus!

Praise God!

Place Card
Instructions

Write Name Here

1. Cut a circle 3-4 inches in diameter.
2. Cut on dotted line as shown in diagram.
3. Pull around and glue on dotted area.
4. Glue small piece of yarn on top.

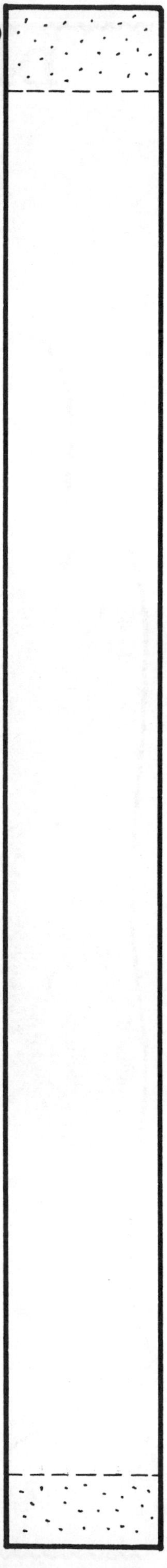

Glue head-
band here
to fit head.

SS1815

DECORATIONS
PRAYING HANDS AND PARTY HATS

1. Cut out 2 hands.
2. Put together to make praying hands.
3. Staple together with the ends of 6 very long streamers of crepe paper in between the hands.
4. Hang praying hands from center of room.
5. Twist streamers and pull to edge of room.
6. Tape ends to wall with mini party hat (shown below).
7. Write words or phrases on the hats that help to spread God's word.
(Examples of words: Love, Forgive, Peace, Happy New Year, etc.)

Decorate with praying hands and party hats!

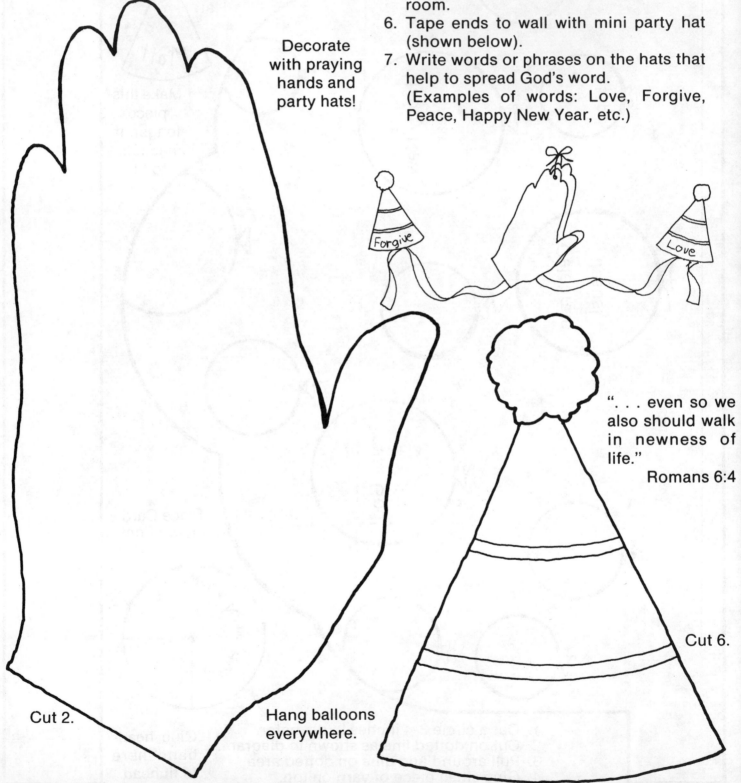

". . . even so we also should walk in newness of life."

Romans 6:4

Cut 2.

Hang balloons everywhere.

Cut 6.

SS1815

CRAFT
TISSUE PAPER CONFETTI HOLDER

1. Give each child a small cardboard cylinder. (Example: empty toilet paper roll or paper towel roll which has been cut in half.)

2. Fill cylinder with small bits of brightly colored paper. Include a small piece of paper in each with a message written on it praising God.

3. Roll cylinder in tissue paper and glue along edge.

4. Tie ends of tissue paper with string or yarn.

5. Save for midnight. When the New Year begins, tear and pull end. Spread confetti in the air to celebrate!

GAMES

NOISY BALLOON RELAY

You will need at least two teams of four players each, a balloon for each player, and two black markers for each team.

1. Divide the number of players on each team equally. Put half of the team at one end and the other half at the other end, and have the team players face each other for the relay.

2. The first player of each team begins by blowing up a balloon.

3. When the balloon is blown up, the player runs to the opposite team member.

4. The opposite team member takes the black marker and writes Happy New Year on the balloon.

5. The original team member must sit on a balloon until it pops.

6. The team member with the marker takes a turn next and follows the same procedure.

7. The relay team to finish first wins the game.

CATCH FATHER TIME GAME

In this game there is only one Father Time. Throughout the game Father Time rings a bell and repeatedly says, "The old year is out. Ring the new year in." All the other players are blindfolded, and they all try to catch Father Time. The one who does trades places with him, and the game continues.

WHAT'S IN THE BAG?

On twelve small paper sacks print one letter of HAPPY NEW YEAR. Place an object that begins with each letter inside each sack. Line the sacks up so that they spell out HAPPY NEW YEAR. Give each child a card with the letters HAPPY NEW YEAR printed on it vertically. Have each child feel the objects without looking inside the sacks. Then, have them write what they think is in each sack. The winner is the one who gets the most correct answers.

CELEBRATE JESUS IN THE NEW YEAR

Have the children walk around in a circle, in the center of which "It" stands blindfolded. When "It" stomps three times on the floor, all the players stand still. "It" points in any direction saying, "Celebrate Jesus." The one "It" is pointing toward answers, "in the new year." If "It" can identify the one who answered, they trade places. If not, the players move around the circle again.

BILLBOARD ADVERTISEMENTS TO CELEBRATE JESUS

Divide the children into small groups of 3 to 4. Provide each group with a large piece of white butcher paper about 3 feet long and a box of water-based markers. Tell the children to design advertisements to Celebrate Jesus and the New Year. When the children have finished, display and show off all the billboards. Be sure to give each billboard equal amounts of praise!

FAVORS
CELEBRATE JESUS DOOR MESSAGE

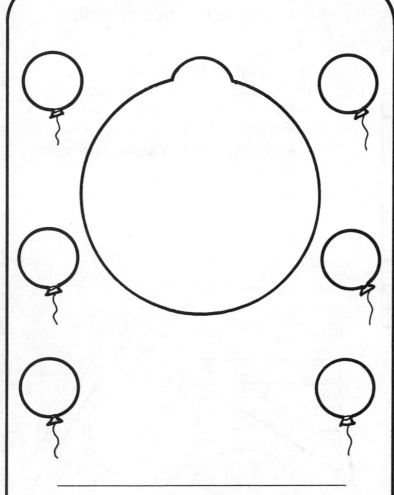

will
celebrate
JESUS
throughout
the
NEW YEAR

1. Reproduce a door message for each child.

2. Have the children cut out and color their own door message.

3. Have each child write his/her own name on the line drawn.

4. Ask the children to take their door messages home and to hang them on a door as a reminder to Celebrate Jesus Throughout the New Year!

"...they were baptized in the name of the Lord Jesus."

Acts 19:5

SS1815

REFRESHMENTS
HAPPY NEW YEAR GOODIES

NEW YEAR FROSTY DRINK

Place in blender:
  ½ cup low fat milk
  ½ cup root beer soda pop
Add: 3 to 4 ice cubes
Mix until frothy.

Poor into tall plastic cup and enjoy!

BALLOON SANDWICHES

Cut out circles of bread with a round cookie cutter to represent shape of balloon. Make sandwiches with your favorite filling—peanut butter, tuna, etc.
Arrange the sandwiches on a tray to look like balloons. Use licorice to dangle from each.

MELTED CHEESE AND CHIPS

Serve each child a small paper cup of melted Velveeta cheese and a serving of your favorite chips.

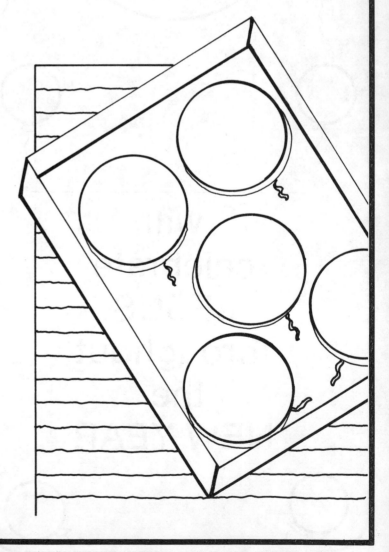

SS1815

Celebrate Jesus throughout the New Year by eating healthy!
Here are some suggestions for healthy snacks to serve at your Happy New Year party.

FRUIT STICKS

Serve toothpick snacks with a piece of pineapple, a bite of banana, and a red cherry stuck through the toothpick.

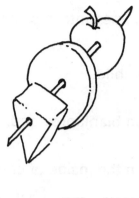

YUMMY GRANOLA COOKIES

Cream:
    ½ cup shortening
    ¼ cup peanut butter
    1 cup brown sugar
    1 egg
    ¼ cup water
    1 teaspoon vanilla

Add:
    1 cup flour
    ½ teaspoon soda

Mix well; stir in 3 cups granola.

Grease cookie sheet.
Bake at 350 degrees for 12 minutes.

Also set out a large tray of carrots, cauliflower, grapes, etc. Serve salad dressings and/or cream cheese as dips!

YUM!

                    SS1815

GOD MADE YOU SPECIAL HAPPY BIRTHDAY IDEAS

Invitation:

". . . Suffer the little children to come unto me, and forbid them not: for of such is the kingdom of God."   Mark 10:14

1. Reproduce an invitation for each child.
2. Cut out and color.
3. Write the birthday child's name on blank provided.
4. Fold on dotted line.
5. Write the following information on the inside of card:

   Where _____ Date _____

   When From _____ Until _____

   RSVP
   Regrets Only—Phone
   _____

Happy
Birthday
To

_____

HATS

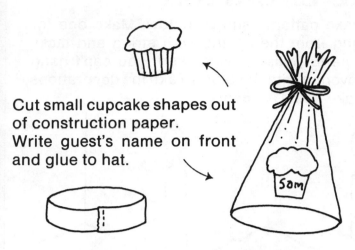

Cut small cupcake shapes out of construction paper.
Write guest's name on front and glue to hat.

1. Make a tube out of cardboard or heavy poster board 2"-3" wide and long enough to fit around the child's head.
2. Take a sheet of brightly colored crepe paper about 12" wide and long enough to fit around the headband with a little left over.
3. Glue, tape, or staple the crepe paper along the seam and around the headband to fit snugly. (Be sure to leave just enough to tuck under edge of headband and glue.)
4. At the top of the crepe paper hat, bring together, twist slightly, and tie with yarn or brightly colored string.

PLACE CARDS

1. Reproduce enough boy/girl place cards for children coming to party.
2. Cut out and color.
3. Write child's name on line provided.
4. Fold on dotted lines.
5. Glue dotted area to back of place card and stand up.

My name is ___
and I am special because God made me!

My name is ___
and I am special because God made me!

SS1815

DECORATIONS
GOD'S SPECIAL CREATION

Enlarge the special candle and special cupcake patterns shown below. Make one for each guest and write his/her name on it. Hang from the ceiling with string and tacks to serve as decorations during the party. (Tape to walls or windows if you can't hang them, but be careful not to damage your wall covering with the tape.) Take the decorations down at the end of the party and hand out to take home as favors.

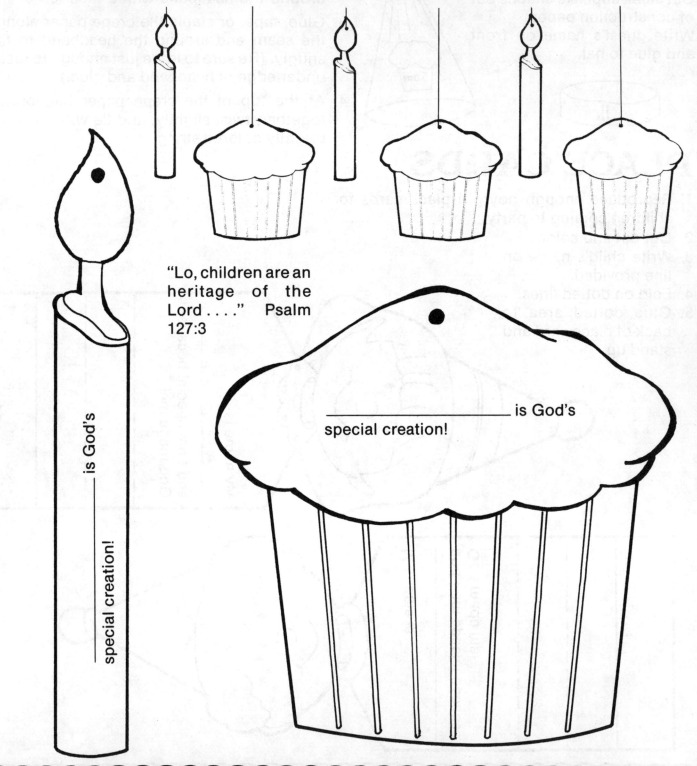

"Lo, children are an heritage of the Lord . . . ." Psalm 127:3

_____ is God's special creation!

_____ is God's special creation!

SS1815

GAMES

GOD'S SPECIAL ONE

Form a circle. Throw a rubber ball high into the air and at the same time, call one of the children's names. The child with that name must catch the ball while everyone else walks quickly away from the circle. (No one may run!) After catching the ball, It yells "stop." Everyone must stop where they are. "It" may take four giant steps toward anyone and try to hit that person with the ball. The player may try to dodge the ball but may not move his/her feet.

If hit, the player becomes "God's Special One," and must then throw the ball for the next turn. If "It" misses, let him/her take four more steps toward another person and try again. If "It" misses again, call another name and begin again.

SPECIAL EGG TOSS

Kids always love the thrill of an egg toss. Make this egg toss a little more suspenseful by adding a hard-boiled egg. Divide your guests into teams of two each. Give each team one egg. Have them face off about two to three feet away from each other and toss the egg. Each time the egg is tossed, have each partner take one step away from each other and toss again until all the eggs have been broken. Explain from the beginning that one egg is special and has been hard-boiled. Players will not know until the end of the game who was lucky enough to draw the special egg.

SS1815

FAVORS
EMBROIDERED CARDS

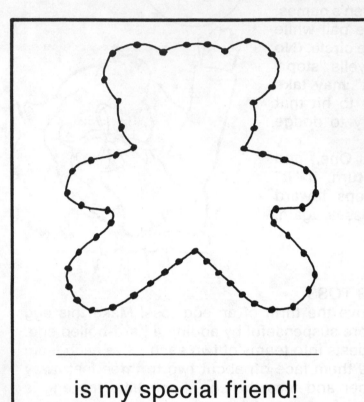

is my special friend!

Materials needed:
needle
yarn or thread
scissors
medium weight cardboard or
poster board

1. Reproduce the patterns shown on medium weight cardboard or poster board.

2. Thread needle with colored yarn or thread and tie a knot in the end.

3. Push threaded needle in and out of black dots that form the pictures.

4. Write guest name on line provided on card.

5. Give one to each guest as party favor!

"Then were there brought unto him little children, that he should put his hands on them, and pray: . . ."

Matthew 19:13

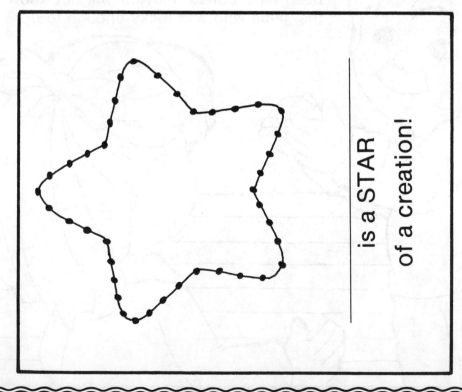

is a STAR
of a creation!

SS1815

REFRESHMENTS
STAR OF A CREATION CAKE

Have the birthday child choose his/her favorite cake and icing flavor and use your own recipes (or boxed cake and icing mix) to make the birthday cake. Patterns below show you how to arrange the Star of a Creation Birthday Cake!

1. Use two large round cake pans at least 9" × 1½" in size. Bake the cake, cool, and remove from pans.

2. Cut one round layer in the shape of an equilateral pentagon (a polygon with five sides of the same length). See the diagram shown. (The pattern of the actual size of the pentagon for a 9" × 1½" cake can be found on the following page.)

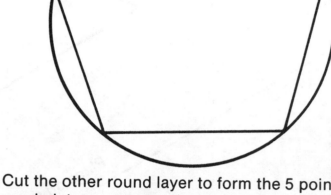

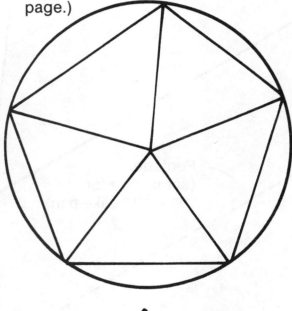

3. Cut the other round layer to form the 5 points needed to construct the star. See diagram shown. (The pattern of the actual size of one point to be cut from a 9" × 1½" layer can be found on the following page.)

4. See the diagram that shows how to arrange the pieces that form the star.

5. Ice the cake and use a decorator tube or can with decorating tips to write a message on the cake.

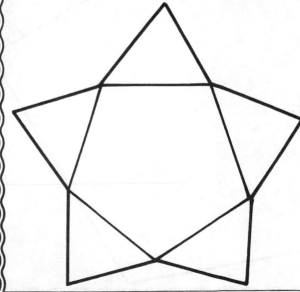

Shining Star Publications, Copyright © 1989, A division of Good Apple, Inc.   SS1815

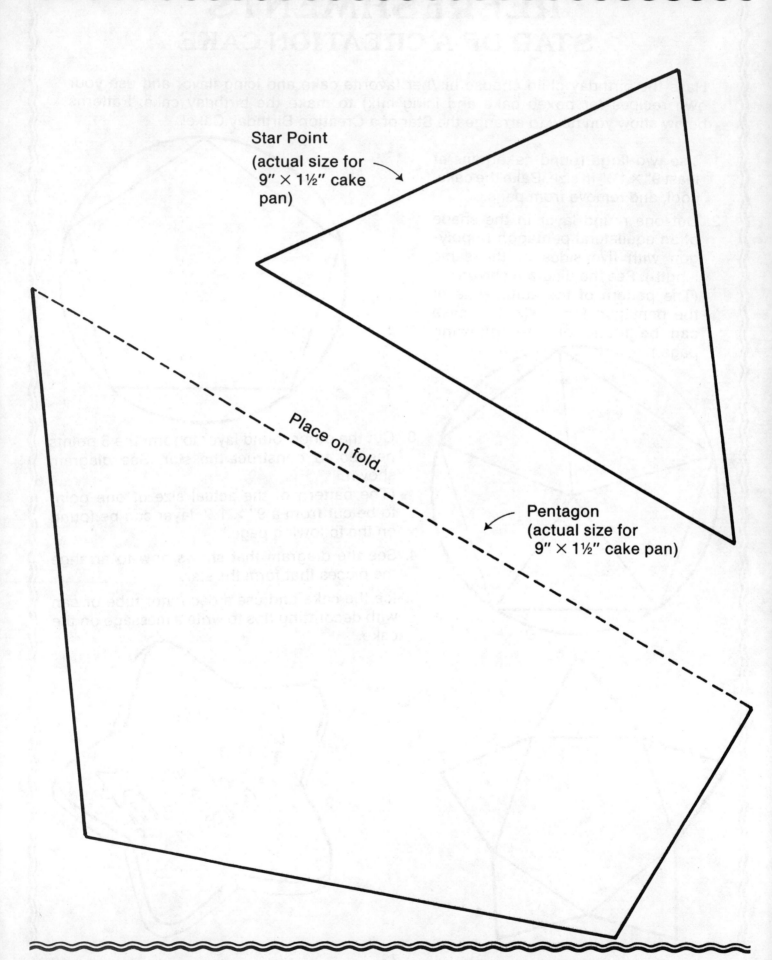

Star Point
(actual size for
9″ × 1½″ cake
pan)

Place on fold.

Pentagon
(actual size for
9″ × 1½″ cake pan)

SS1815

MARTIN LUTHER KING, JR.
CELEBRATION

(Martin Luther King, Jr.—Birthday—January 18)

LOVE THY NEIGHBOR

"A new commandment I give unto you, That ye love one another; as I have loved you, that ye also love one another."   John 13:34

Directions:

1. Reproduce and color.
2. Cut out.
3. Fold on dotted line to make a card.
4. Write the following message on the inside of invitation:

You are invited to a
Martin Luther King, Jr. Celebration.
Love Thy Neighbor!

Given By _____

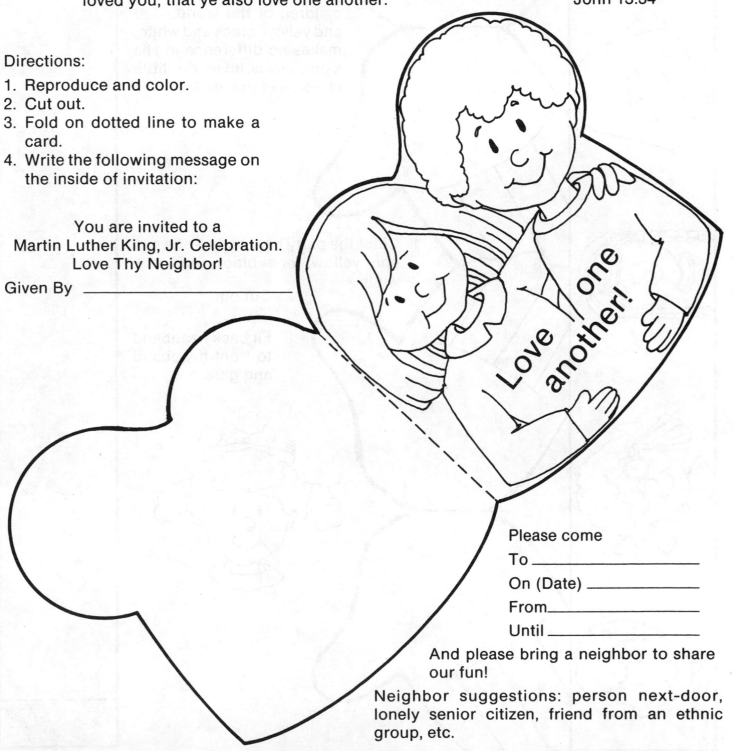

Love one another!

Please come

To _____

On (Date) _____

From_____

Until _____

And please bring a neighbor to share our fun!

Neighbor suggestions: person next-door, lonely senior citizen, friend from an ethnic group, etc.

SS1815

HATS

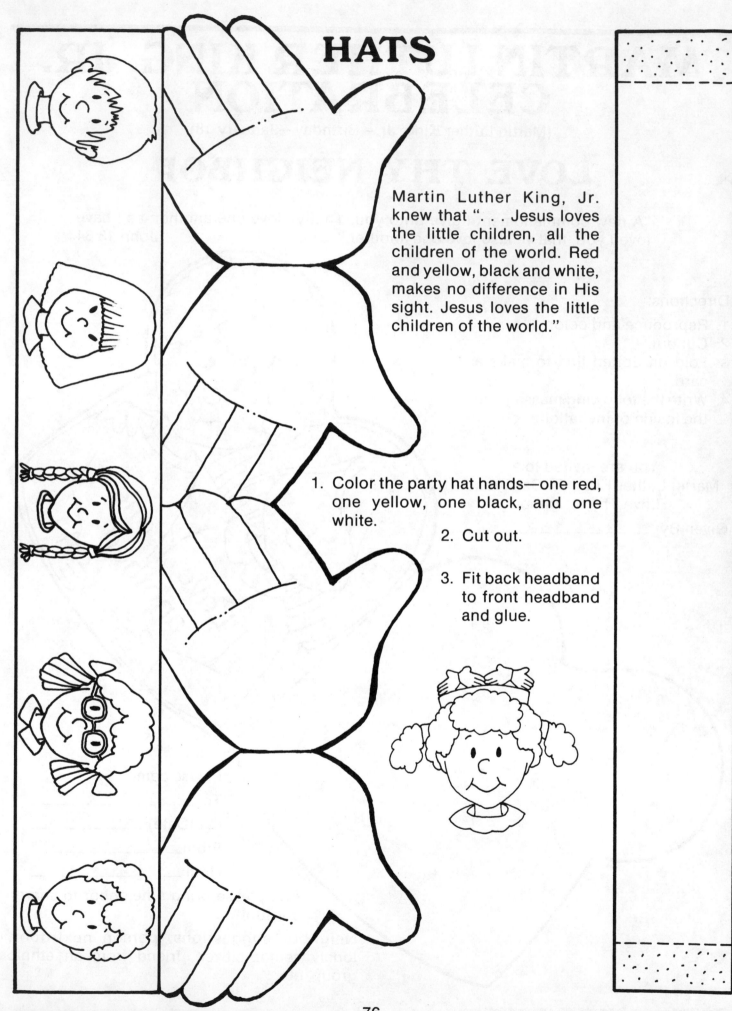

Martin Luther King, Jr. knew that ". . . Jesus loves the little children, all the children of the world. Red and yellow, black and white, makes no difference in His sight. Jesus loves the little children of the world."

1. Color the party hat hands—one red, one yellow, one black, and one white.

2. Cut out.

3. Fit back headband to front headband and glue.

SS1815

DECORATIONS

"... but thou shalt love thy neighbour as thyself: I am the Lord."

Leviticus 19:18

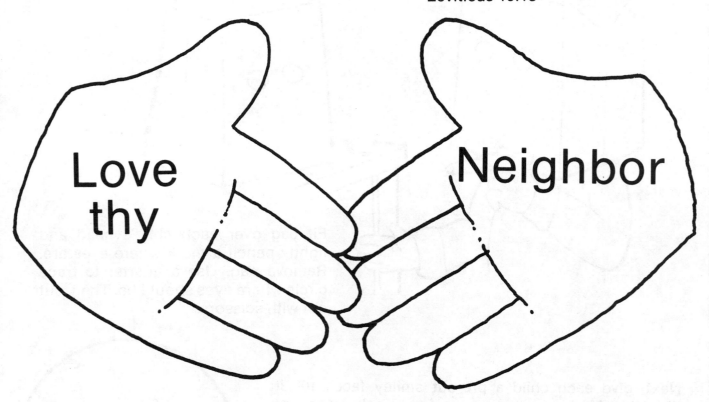

1. Enlarge and reproduce the "Love Thy Neighbor" hands for every two people coming to the celebration.

2. Color and cut out.

3. Use colored poster board to cut out letters of names of people invited to party.

4. Tie the letters together to form the names.

5. Hang the letters from the hands as shown in diagram. Then, hang from ceiling or from doorways for decorations.

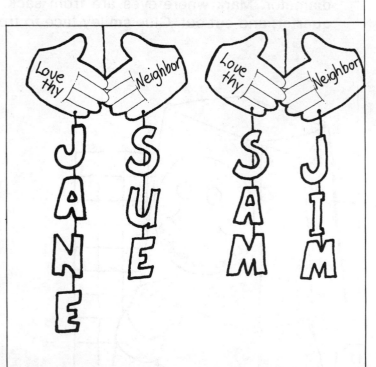

SS1815

CRAFT
SMILEY FACE PAPER BAGS

Give each child a large paper sack.

Fit bag over each child's head and lightly pencil a mark where eyes are. Remove bag. Use a quarter to trace circle where eyes should be. Then, cut out with scissors.

Next, give each child a pre-cut smiley face—10" in diameter. Mark where eyes are from sack, trace with quarter, and cut out. Glue smiley face to front of sack.

Now that the children have prepared their sacks, have them put them on over their heads so that everyone looks alike.

They are ready now to play Paper Bag Puppet Guessing Game on the next page.

SS1815

GAMES

PAPER BAG PUPPET GUESSING GAME

Have the children wear their paper bag puppet heads. Tape a number to each child's shirt. Give each child a pencil and a tablet with numbers 1 through the number of guests at the party written on the tablet. Mix the children up. Have the children approach each other. Instruct each child to try and recognize their friends and without talking, write their names on the tablet by the number that corresponds to the number taped to their shirts. The game is over when everyone's list is complete.

A FORM OF CHARADES

Divide the children into groups of two. Have each group take a turn in acting out a well-known Bible phrase, a song title, the name of a famous peacemaker, etc. Since we are celebrating Martin Luther King, Jr., it would be good to select those things or people that help to promote the idea of Love Thy Neighbor. If the children are very young, you might want to go over the list of answers before you play the game. Then they can guess which one is being acted out. Some suggestions might be: Love Thy Neighbor, "Jesus Loves the Little Children," Martin Luther King, Jr., "We Are the World," The Good Samaritan, and "Jesus Loves Me."

THE EYES HAVE IT

Choose one person to be "It." Have the other children line up with their eyes closed. "It" must try to guess each person's eye color. After "It" has guessed a color, have all the children open their eyes to see if "It" is correct. Keep a record of how many correct guesses "It" makes.

As each child's turn is complete, divide the children into eye color groups. After the game is completed, it should be interesting to see how many have blue eyes, brown eyes, etc.

Even though our skin may be different in color, we may share the same eye color with our "neighbor." Remember—Love Thy Neighbor! We're not so different, after all!

   SS1815

FAVORS
LOVE ONE ANOTHER
AUTOGRAPH BOOK

Reproduce one extra invitation for each guest. Add 4-5 sheets of colored paper the same shape as the card to inside. Staple along the edge to make an autograph book.
Hand them out along with pencils toward the end of your party and have the children collect each other's autographs. This is a good way to promote friendship!

PORTRAIT OF A NEIGHBOR

You will need:
1. Drawing paper 9"×12" or larger
2. Pencils
3. Markers
4. Yarn (for eyebrows and hair)
5. Scraps of material (for collars of clothes)
6. Pairs of blue, brown, and green buttons (for eyes)
7. Glue

"Devise not evil against thy neighbour, . . ."
Proverbs 3:29

1. Divide the children by twos.

2. Give each child drawing paper and pencil. Have them sketch a life-size, front-view portrait of each other.

3. Give each one yarn, colored buttons for eyes, and scraps of material and instruct the children to complete the picture.

4. When completed, give each child his/her own portrait to take home

Shining Star Publications, Copyright © 1989, A division of Good Apple, Inc.   SS1815

REFRESHMENTS

DRINK:

Before the party pour grape, orange, lime, or strawberry soft drink into an ice cube tray and freeze.

When it's time to serve refreshments, put the colored ice cubes in see-through glasses or plastic cups and pour a contrasting color of soft drink over the cubes.

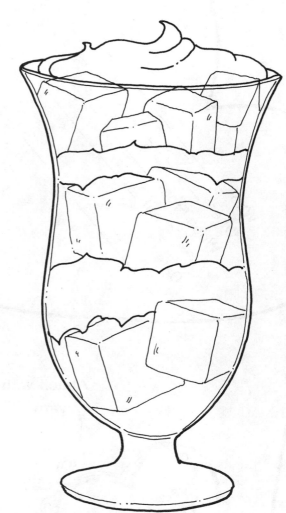

GELATIN DESSERT:

Pour 1-3 oz. package of gelatin (any colorful fruit flavor) into one cup boiling water. Dissolve. Pour dissolved gelatin and ¾ cup cold water into 9″ square pan. Chill until firmly set. Cut into cubes. Dip pan into warm water, invert, and empty cubes onto waxed paper.

Alternate layers of 3-4 cubes of gelatin and layers of non-dairy whipped topping in tall see-through glasses or plastic containers.

SERVE AND ENJOY!

GREAT!   YUM!

SS1815

VALENTINE'S DAY

(February 14th)

"Be kindly affectioned one to another with brotherly love; . . ."

Romans 12:10

Directions:

1. Reproduce one for each guest.
2. Color.
3. Cut out on dark line.
4. Punch hole and attach with yarn. (See diagram.)
5. Fill in information and hand out.

"Jesus Loves Me This I Know" Party

Who _____
Where _____
When From _____ Until _____

Date _____

RSVP Card
Name _____
Circle yes or no and please return.

Attach with yarn

"Jesus Loves Me This I Know" Party

SS1815

HATS
AND PLACE CARDS

1. Color. 2. Cut out on dark line (3 per hat). 3. Staple to fit.

toothpick

Cut three.
(Glue or staple
sides to fit head.)

Cut heart from
poster board.

JESUS
LOVES
TIM

John

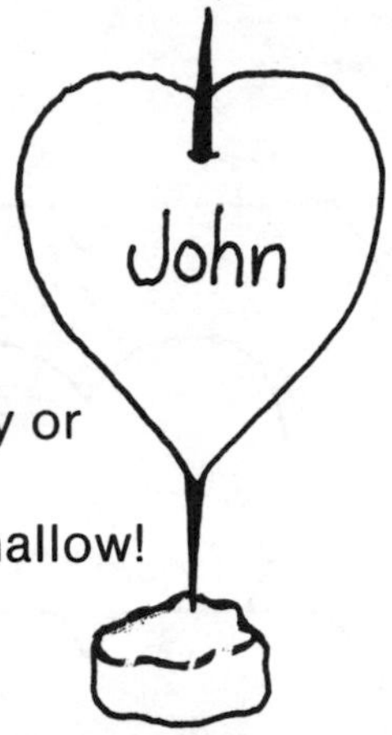

Use clay or
a large
marshmallow!

Jesus
Loves

_____

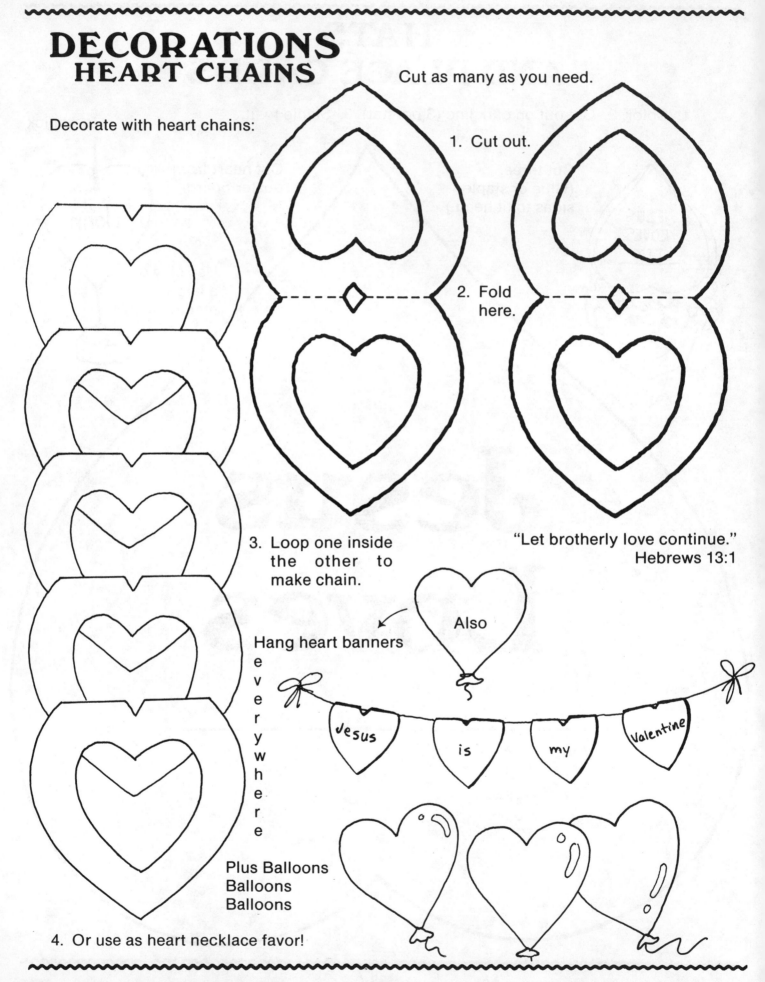

DECORATIONS
HEART CHAINS

Cut as many as you need.

Decorate with heart chains:

1. Cut out.

2. Fold here.

3. Loop one inside the other to make chain.

"Let brotherly love continue."
Hebrews 13:1

Also

Hang heart banners

e v e r y w h e r e

Jesus is my Valentine

Plus Balloons
Balloons
Balloons

4. Or use as heart necklace favor!

Shining Star Publications, Copyright © 1989, A division of Good Apple, Inc.   SS1815

GAMES AND CRAFTS

JESUS LOVES ME—Musical Chairs: (Good for younger and older children.)

Place chairs (one for each child) in a circle. Have children march around the chairs singing "Jesus Loves Me." Remove one chair at a time as the children circle around. When you yell "STOP," children stop singing and scramble to sit in a chair. A child is left out each time. Continue until all but one child is out.

VARIATION:
Leave all chairs in the circle. Tape a heart shape under one chair. When the music stops, and children sit down, the one sitting on the heart wins a prize. Be sure to change the place of the heart each time. (It is a nice idea to give everyone a prize at the end of the game whether they have won or not.)

CRAFTS:
Share the love Jesus has blessed us with by making and exchanging valentines at your party.
Provide plenty of red and white construction paper, markers, and enough heart-shaped patterns for everyone to have one for tracing hearts. Some suggestions:

Note: Have candy wrapped be-fore gluing.

MATCH THE HEARTS

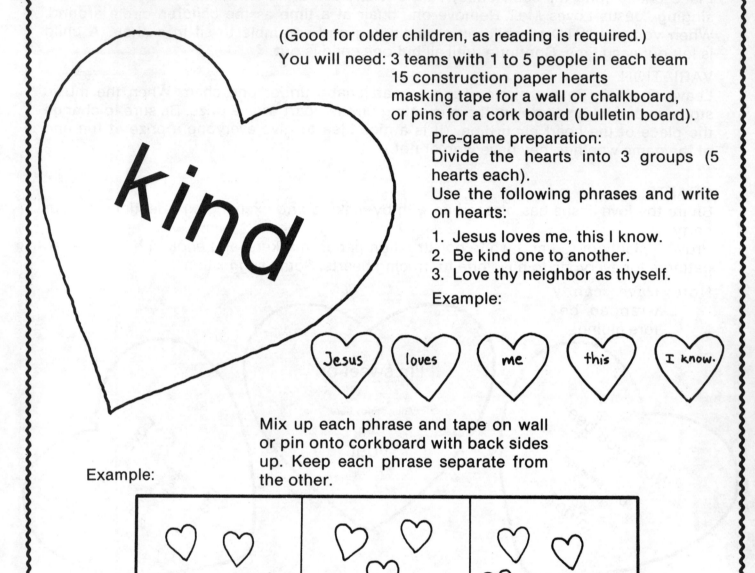

(Good for older children, as reading is required.)

You will need: 3 teams with 1 to 5 people in each team
15 construction paper hearts
masking tape for a wall or chalkboard,
or pins for a cork board (bulletin board).

Pre-game preparation:
Divide the hearts into 3 groups (5 hearts each).
Use the following phrases and write on hearts:

1. Jesus loves me, this I know.
2. Be kind one to another.
3. Love thy neighbor as thyself.

Example:

Mix up each phrase and tape on wall or pin onto corkboard with back sides up. Keep each phrase separate from the other.

Example:

To play game:

Each team member goes to board one at a time. When it is your turn, you may select one heart. Turn it over and read it. If you think it is the next word in a phrase, tape it right side up at bottom of board for your team to see. If not, return it to board with back side up and return to your team. Next person repeats instructions. The first team to complete the phrase wins the game. (Add any number of teams and phrases to accommodate the number of people at your party.)

FAVORS
JESUS LOVES YOU CANDY CUP

1. Reproduce and color.
2. Cut out.
3. Fold on dotted lines and paste flaps inside to form the cup.
4. Fill each cup with heart-shaped candies and give as party favors or prizes. (Be sure everyone gets a prize. There are no such things as losers.)

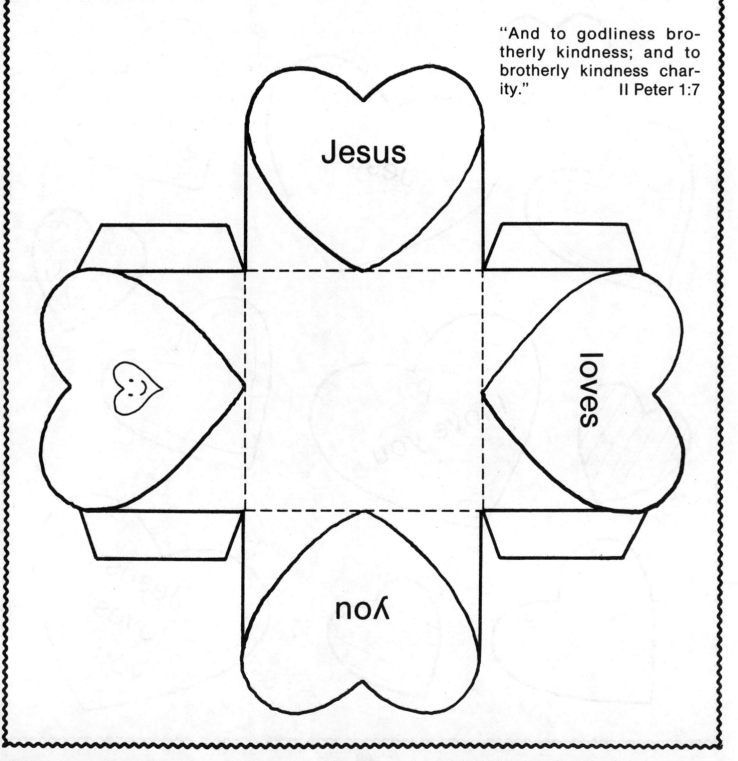

"And to godliness brotherly kindness; and to brotherly kindness charity."
II Peter 1:7

SS1815

VALENTINE STICKER SHEET

1. Reproduce one copy for each guest:
2. Mix equal amounts of Elmer's Glue, or Lepage's Mucilage and water together in a small container.
3. Use a paintbrush and apply the glue mixture to the back of each sticker page.
4. Let the pages dry completely, glue side up.
5. Give as favors at party.
6. Guests may color and decorate stickers. Then, cut out, dampen back, and stick!

SS1815

REFRESHMENTS
VALENTINE PARTY
YUM-YUMS

LOVE PUNCH

4 liters strawberry flavored (or any red flavor) carbonated soft drink

2 liters ginger ale

1/2 gallon pineapple sherbert, vanilla ice cream, or any other flavor of your choice

Mix strawberry flavored drink and ginger ale in large punch bowl. Add sherbert or ice cream and leave in chunks. May double the recipe for larger parties.

Serve to smiling valentine faces!

JESUS LOVES YOU COOKIES

2/3 cup shortening
3/4 cup granulated sugar
1 teaspoon vanilla
1 egg
4 teaspoons milk
1 1/2 teaspoons baking powder
1/4 teaspoon salt
2 cups flour

Cream shortening, sugar, and vanilla. Add egg and beat. Stir in milk.

Sift together baking powder, salt, and flour. Blend into creamed mixture.

Divide dough and chill at least one hour. After chilling, roll out and cut using heart-shaped cookie cutters. Bake on greased cookie sheet at 375 degrees for 6 to 8 minutes.

A DROP OF LOVE ICING

1 cup shortening
1 teaspoon vanilla
4 cups sifted confectioners' sugar
1 1/2 tablespoons milk

Blend shortening and vanilla. Slowly add sifted confectioners' sugar. Beat to mix. Stir in milk. If frosting is too stiff, add more milk.

Ice cookies with white icing. Save a third of the icing and color with a few drops of red food coloring. Use a pastry tube (or waxed paper) to decorate cookies with "Jesus Loves You"!

SS1815

CELEBRATE JONAH

"Now the Lord had prepared a great fish to swallow up Jonah. And Jonah was in the belly of the fish three days and three nights."

Jonah 1:17

Directions:
1. Reproduce one for each guest.
2. Color.
3. Cut out.
4. Glue flap to dotted area.
5. Cut slot and slip in flap to close mouth.
6. Hand out to guests.

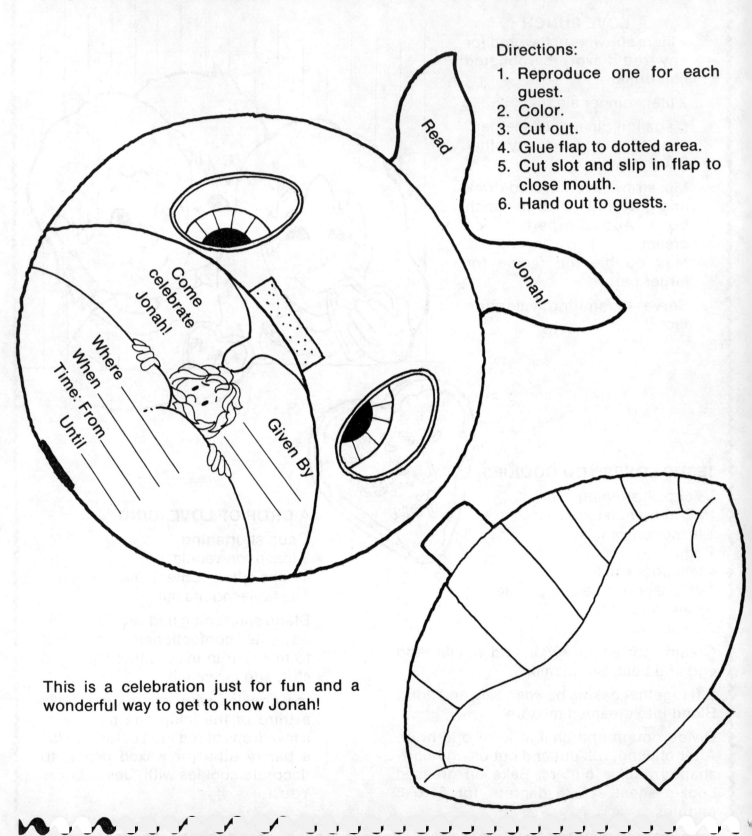

Read

Jonah!

Come celebrate Jonah!

Where _____
When _____
Time: From _____
Until _____

Given By

This is a celebration just for fun and a wonderful way to get to know Jonah!

HATS

1. Reproduce one for each guest.
2. Color.
3. Cut out.
4. Glue back headband to front headband to fit.

PLACE CARDS

Reproduce 6 sea animal shapes for each child. Fill in child's name on all 6 shapes. Tape or glue to a plastic drinking cup. Arrange around table.

Celebrate Jonah

Name _____

Name _____

Name _____

Name _____

back headband

SS1815

PLACE MATS

1. Enlarge pattern to place mat size or attach to a place mat sized sheet of paper.
2. Color.
3. Cut out.
4. Arrange around table.

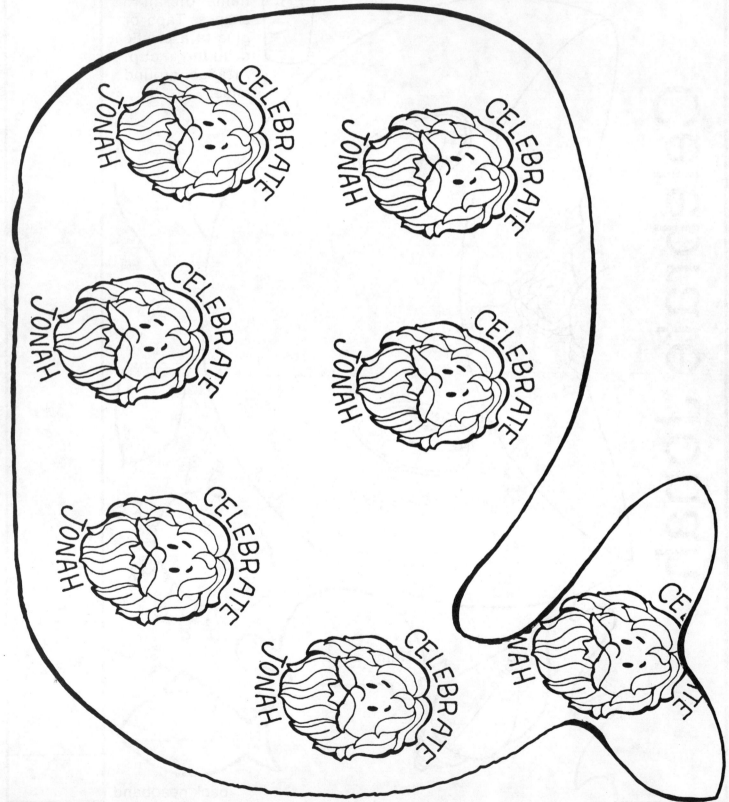

                                          SS1815

ACTIVITY
JONAH CHORAL READING

Have your guests make hose-and-hanger puppets and perform the Jonah Choral Reading for their parents. (See next two pages for patterns and instructions for hose-and-hanger puppets.)

Jonah:	The Lord called to me and asked me to go.
Sea Animals:	But Jonah ran off and told the Lord no.
Jonah:	I ran to the sea and hid on a boat.
Sea Animals:	Was thrown overboard. It's good he could float.
Whale:	The Lord sent me to swallow Jonah whole.
Jonah:	I was being punished because I said no.
Sea Animals:	He prayed to the Lord for three days and three nights.
Jonah:	I said I was sorry, and I saw the light.
Whale:	I spit Jonah up and onto the shore.
Sea Animals:	The Lord forgave Jonah forevermore.

"Then Jonah prayed unto the Lord his God out of the fish's belly,"   Jonah 2:1

SS1815

HOSE-AND-HANGER PUPPETS

Instructions:
1. Round out a hanger to form head shape.
2. Slip hosiery over hanger, attach at bottom with rubber band, and cut off excess.
3. Enlarge and trace patterns shown onto construction paper and glue to hose and hanger.

Be sure everyone has a part!

Note: Cover end of hanger with cotton ball for safety.

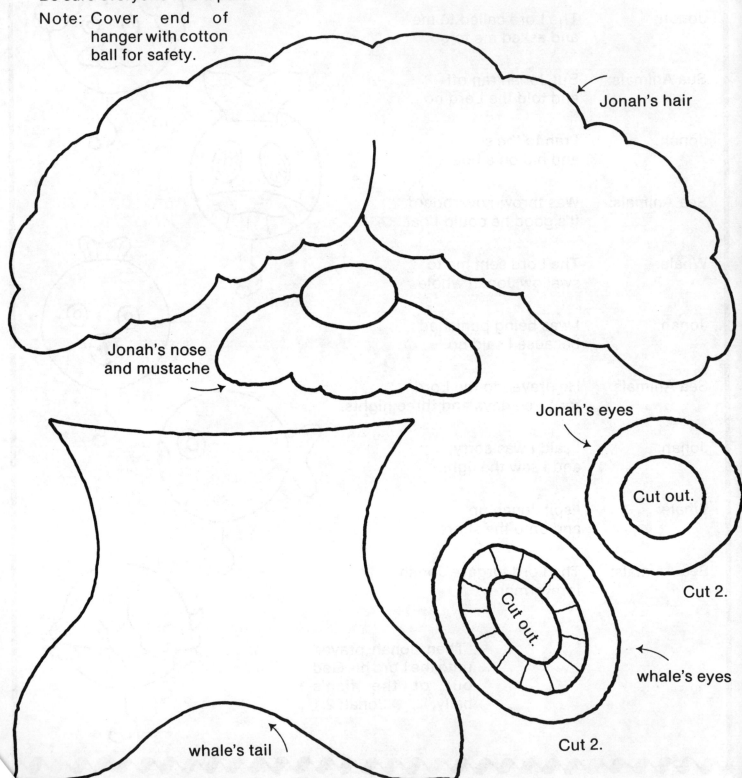

Jonah's hair

Jonah's nose and mustache

Jonah's eyes

Cut out.

Cut 2.

Cut out.

whale's eyes

Cut 2.

whale's tail

SS1815

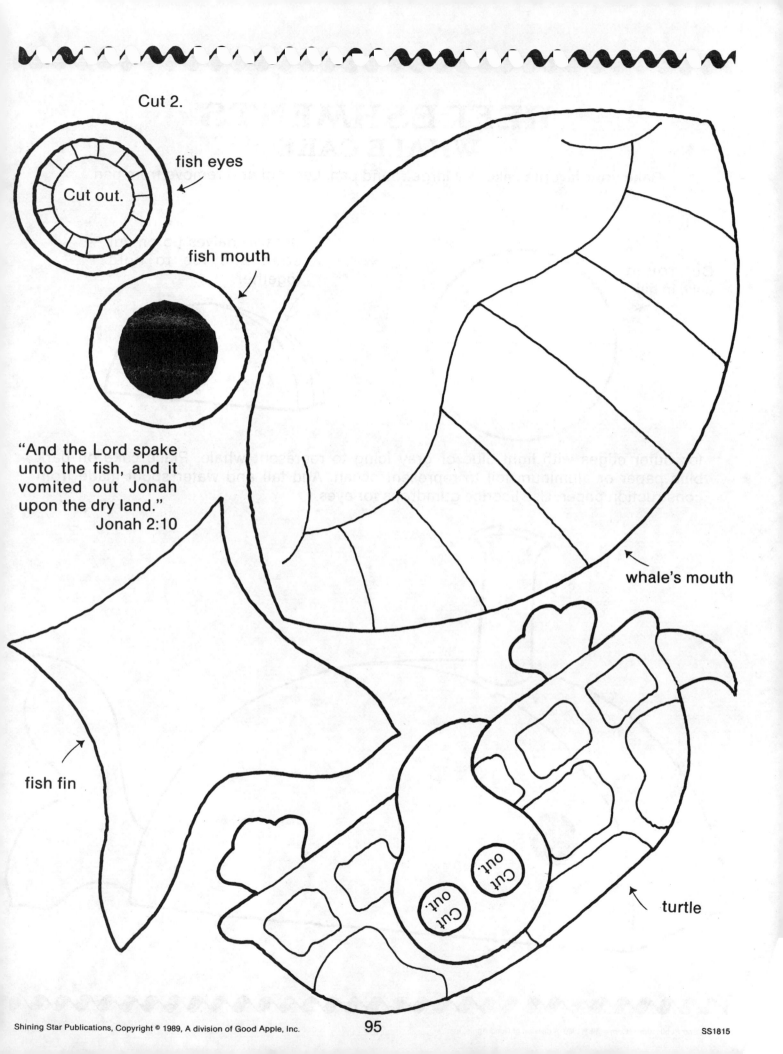

Cut 2.

fish eyes

Cut out.

fish mouth

"And the Lord spake unto the fish, and it vomited out Jonah upon the dry land."
Jonah 2:10

whale's mouth

fish fin

Cut out.

Cut out.

turtle

SS1815

REFRESHMENTS
WHALE CAKE

Bake your favorite cake in a large round pan. Let cool and remove from pan.

Cut round cake in half.

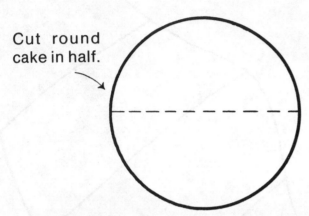

Set two halves up on cut edge and ice to hold together.

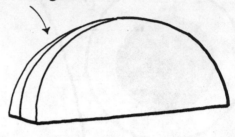

Ice outer edges with light blue or gray icing to represent whale. Place cake on dark blue paper or aluminum foil to represent ocean. Add tail and water spout made from construction paper. Use licorice gumdrops for eyes.

hing Star Publications, Copyright © 1989, A division of Good Apple, Inc.